# Mockingbird Dance

*Love Takes Flight in Amish Country*

## Karen Anna Vogel

Lamb Books

*Hope is the thing with feathers that perches in the soul - and sings the tunes without the words - and never stops at all.*
EMILY DICKINSON

# Contents

# Amish-English

## Dictionary

*How Pennsylvania Dutch overflows into Western Pennsylvanian slang.*

To be or not to be, that is the question. Folks in Western PA, along with local Amish, do not use "to be". It's not, "The car needs *to be* washed." We simply say, "The car needs washed." This is only one example. This book is full of similar "grammar errors" but tries to be authentic to how people talk in our "neck of the woods".

Ach – oh
Boppli – baby
Daed - dad
Danki – thank you
Dochder -daughter

Gelassenheit - self-surrender, submission, yielding to the will of God and to others, contentment, and a calm spirit. Most important, *Gelassenheit* is the opposite of bold individualism that promotes self-interest at every turn. This is the point where Amish society diverges most significantly from contemporary culture. (Communal Values, Amish Studies, The Young Center.) Communal Values – Amish Studies (etown.edu)

Gmay – community or church
Grosseldre - grandparents
Grosskinner -- grandchildren
Oma - grandmother
Opa - grandfather
Gut – good
Jah - yes
Kapp- cap; Amish women's head covering
Kinner – children

Mamm – mom

Nee- no

Ordnung - A set of rules for Amish, Old Order Mennonite and Conservative Mennonite living. Ordnung is the German word for order, discipline, rule, arrangement, organization, or system.

Rumspringa – running around years, starting at sixteen, when Amish youth experience the outsiders' way of life before joining the church.

Schwester – sister

Schwestern - sisters

Wunderbar – wonderful

Yinz – You all or you two, slang found in Western Pennsylvania among the Amish and those who speak Pittsburghese.

# Chapter 1

Gracie Hershberger never considered herself a beauty, but her beau, Silas Miller, complimented her time and time again, saying no one in the church district compared to her. But, *Mamm* always said, it's the inner beauty that counts. *Mamm* had told her she'd had that in abundance. "You have a smile that warms me right through," she'd said. "The way you cool my head when a fever comes, it's like being touched by an angel above. A real angel you are to me, and the whole family."

Gracie pulled back the white curtain to view the sunrise as the coffee percolated on the woodstove. Through the bare tree limbs, she could see it in all its glory. Magenta swirled across the eastern sky behind white clouds.

*Help me, Lord. It's only been five days and I miss my Mamm so. It was an honor to care for her and hold her hand as she left this earth for heaven, but I never expected to feel such raw emptiness. It's like reliving Daed's departure three years ago. Death is so final. Too final. But I'll do my best to follow Mamm's instructions to always stay on God's path, no matter if sometimes it leaves you with more questions than answers.*

A mockingbird at the platform feeder danced as the sun burst upon the horizon. *Help me be like that bird. It's so cheerful...*

An Amish buggy appeared and pulled into the driveway. She soon made out that it was her two sisters. They'd have sticky buns and pie for breakfast, just for a change. Soon, the two sisters were greeting Gracie at the front door. The sisters embraced, biting back tears. Gracie didn't need to ask why. *Mamm's* presence had vanished.

"Danki for the pies, Rachel. And Teresa, sticky buns are always a treat."

They took their usual seats at the family table as Gracie poured coffee.

"Are you still too tired to bake?" Rachel asked. "I don't smell peach cobbler."

Gracie opened her icebox. "Look, I have desserts to give away. How about sponge cake?"

Rachel pouted. "But, you know I crave peach pie when I'm pregnant—"

"Sponge cake is fine, Gracie," Teresa interrupted.

"Rachel, our *schwester* is tired. Caring for our *Mamm* and the funeral in the house has made her exhausted."

"*Ach,* I'm just concerned," Rachel went on. "You look so pale."

Gracie disregarded her comments, knowing she had no understanding of the effort it took to care for *mamm* and clean up after mourners. Of course, she was there, but was allergic to using the broom somehow. Gracie turned to pour the coffee. *Will Rachel and I ever be close?* She dished dessert onto plates and soon they were sipping coffee and munching on sweets.

"Despite the large turnout at the funeral, it was heartwarming to see many Ohio cousins," Teresa remarked.

"*Jah*, it was nice for once to see them wear black like they should," Rachel mentioned. "We're true to the Amish way, wearing only black and blue."

"Bruises are black and blue," Gracie let slip. "I mean, well, what's wrong with green? Trees are green and pansies are purple."

Teresa grinned. "Gracie, you say out loud what we all think. I hope someday we can wear green like the Smicksburg Amish wear."

Rachel fanned herself with a napkin, looking faint. "Do you think Silas will pop the big question now?"

"He did already, *schwester*. A month ago…"

"Did you accept?"

Gracie gulped. "*Nee*, not yet. *Mamm* had some concerns about him. She thinks he wanted the farm more than me."

The sisters gasped in horror. "*Mamm* said that? *Ach*, it was the pain medicines talking," Rachel assured. "I see how Silas looks at you. You've been courting for two years, right?"

Gracie felt heat on her cheeks. "Why he didn't help more when *Daed* died, why he couldn't bear to see *Mamm* in pain, not visiting much, gave me room to suspect a few things." Gracie finished her coffee. "We can go through *Mamm*'s belongings when we're done eating, and you can take what you'd like."

Teresa's face fell. "I just want *Mamm* back. She made my hope chest overflow with things I'll be passing down to my *kinner*. Maybe a quilt we made on a good day. *Jah*, I'd like to remember *Mamm* pain free."

Rachel yanked a handkerchief from her apron pocket. "*Ach,* me, too."

Gracie waited for a spell so the tears could subside. "What about the grandfather clock? And the cuckoo clock? Or the pendulum clock? *Daed*'s collection of clocks is throughout the house. Surely, you want one."

Teresa took Gracie's hand. I wish for this house to

remain unchanged. When we visit, and the clocks chime by pendulum or cuckoos, we'll feel right at home."

"*Jah*," Rachel said. "You and Silas will make this a happy home again. A working farm again?"

Gracie's stomach knotted. She needed to speak up to her older *schwester* concerning Silas. Maybe she didn't want to live in this house forever. Although she loved the clocks, two on each floor, not dozens, would be fine. *Ach*, was this her grief talking?

∞ ∞ ∞

Gracie's nerves were on edge, so she invited her two closest friends over for fellowship and to crochet. Gracie had prepared a table full of desserts when Maryann and Betty arrived.

"There's nothing I can eat," Maryann protested. "My goal is to keep off the ten pounds I've lost."

"I'll try some sponge cake," Betty chirped. "My favorite. Gracie, I got you a little gift."

When the girls hung their capes and hats on pegs, Gracie lifted a statue of an older woman kneeling down to hold her daughter. What was Betty thinking? Amish couldn't make images of people.

"Do you like it? I love Willow Tree statues. They don't have faces and we're allowed to have them."

"Are you sure?"

"*Jah*, my uncle's the bishop, remember?"

Gracie stared at the statue and memories of special times with her *mamm* flooded her heart and a sob escaped. "I, ah, am sorry."

Her two friends enveloped her with a hug as she wept. This is what she needed. Sisters from the heart. "Danki so much."

"We're here for you," Maryann said, leading Gracie to an Amish rocker. "You don't have to be a big, tough girl around us." Maryann kissed the top of Gracie's prayer *kapp*. "Now, how can we help you?"

Gracie motioned for them to take a seat. "I just want some *gut* fellowship. My *schwester* were here this morning and..."

"Let me guess," Betty started. "Teresa was as sweet as pie and Rachel as sour as pickles?"

They knew her family dynamics well. "Rachel keeps pushing me to accept Silas." She pulled gray yarn from her tote. "I'm like the pendulum clocks in this house. One minute I'm in love with Silas, the other I want to run from him."

Maryann cleared her throat. "Well, it's a big decision. I had my doubts when I married Rick. His family didn't like me, as you know, but now we're chummy."

"So, you had doubts?"

"Everyone does," Betty said. "My Paul is, well, so handsome. Half the church district had their eye on him, but not me. When he asked to take me on a buggy ride, it shocked me. We became close, but I wondered if he wasn't so...easy on the eyes, as the English say, would I marry him?"

"What made you realize he was the one?"

Betty beamed. "We talked so freely on our first outing, and it never changed. After a few months, it just seemed natural that we should get married."

"I remember when you two became official, and the tears so many girls shed."

Betty blushed. "Some have told me, that if Paul had to marry anybody, they were glad it was me."

"That's because you're so sweet," Gracie said with feeling. "You're such a *gut* listener. Some say that listening is the best way to express love."

They worked their crochet hooks in silence for a stretch, as the spring rain patted the windows, adding to the calm. Gracie hadn't been this relaxed for months. Or was it a year, ever since *Mamm* took sick? *Mamm* had said they were two peas in a pod, best friends. It touched Gracie's heart, since *Mamm* had many friends.

"What are you thinking about?" Betty asked.

"*Mamm*, as usual. I thought I'd find comfort in keeping her house going, but I miss her all the more. I'm not sure if I want to live here."

"Give each hour to God and the years will take care of themselves. My favorite Amish proverb," Maryann said. "One I'm relying on now. Since I had my *boppli*, my moods are all over the place."

"How is little Sarah?" Betty asked.

"I don't want to put her down at times, other times I wish she'd sleep more."

Betty held up a hand. "I have some news of my own." She stood and smoothed out her dress in the front. "Do you see anything?"

"You're pregnant!" Maryann screamed. "*Ach*, I'm so happy for you."

Although Gracie wanted to cry, she hugged her friend and said she'd be the best *Mamm*. It hurt, considering Gracie's age of twenty-seven. Could she delay deciding to marry Silas? Her biological clock was ticking!

After Sunday service, folk bombarded Gracie with their concern about her. Many said they'd come and sit with her, fearing she'd be too lonely. Amidst widespread loneliness in America, Gracie found solace in her Amish way of life. Despite having reasons to be grateful, why did she have the desire to flee? Be alone?

She persevered through making cold cut sandwiches and serving the men. When it was time for the women to eat, she sneaked out of the Kline's home and ran into the woods behind it. It was a balmy day for a New York spring, and she needed the scent of pine and grass to clear her mind. Was there something wrong with her? When she reached the pond at the edge of the property, she pulled her pocket New Testament out. Speak to me, Lord. I need to be steady. You've always been my anchor and I need you in this storm!

She found Psalm 91, a passage her *mamm* relied upon.

*He that dwelleth in the secret place of the most High shall abide under the shadow of the Almighty. I will say of the Lord, He is my refuge and my fortress: my God; in him will I trust.*

A breeze graced her face as she pondered the words, secret place, refuge, fortress. A lightness lifted her soul. She had security in this storm. A calm yet boldness overwhelmed her.

She continued to read and paused again when she read:

*He shall cover thee with his feathers, and under his wings shalt thou trust:*

Joy bubbled up in her soul. Her *mamm* knew this secret. When she lost her husband to a heart attack, *Mamm* read her Bible more than usual. She'd memorize whole passages and afterward tell her *kinner* she was fine, that she was standing up inside because the Lord was with her.

"And You are with me," Gracie whispered.

Again, a sweet breeze seemed to kiss her cheek.

In that moment, Gracie resolved to dedicate more time to the secret place of the Lord. He'd be like a mother hen, covering her chicks with his wings.

A twig snapped and Gracie jumped. "*Ach,* Silas. What are you doing here?" His handsome face still made her heart flip. What would the children of someone with blue eyes and dark features look like, given her fair complexion? She dismissed the thought.

"I saw you running away. Are you okay?" He sat on the log next to her, putting a protective arm around her. "I'm worried about you."

"I need time alone." She lifted her Bible. "I've needed more time reading this. *Mamm* was right. It's food for the soul."

He chuckled. "You sound like a sidewalk preacher."

Gracie pulled away. "You don't take me seriously. I said I found comfort. I've needed comfort."

He backed away, hands up. "Gracie, don't be so touchy. I was trying to lighten you up. Everyone's worried about you. Your *schwester*, Rachel, paid me a visit, asking if I can help."

Crossing her arms, she blurted. "Rachel had no right."

"Do I have any rights? Gracie, you're my fiancé. Why do I have to hear from your *schwester* that you need help?"

Gracie looked into his deep blue eyes. "Because you never come around. You didn't visit when *Mamm* was sick. You attended the funeral but left before the viewings. That's why you're clueless about my well-being.

Silas lowered his head. "I'm sorry, Gracie. You know I work long hours for my *daed*. When I see him out in the fields, a fear comes over me he'll have a heart attack just like your *daed*." He took Gracie's hands. "When your *mamm* got cancer, I was afraid your house was cursed."

Gracie wanted to roll her eyes, but the panic in Silas' voice was pitiful. "You don't have to be afraid of death. We learned that since we were young. The Lord is in control of everything. "Here, read this. It gives comfort and...courage."

"*Danki*, Gracie. I appreciate it. And sorry for making fun of your cousins. My parents won't talk to our liberal relatives."

He got on one knee and took her hands. "When can we get married? You're so *gut* for me, Gracie."

Gracie heard her *mamm*'s concern reverberate through her mind. He loves the farm more than you. She breathed, trying to clear her mind. What if it were true?

"I'm thinking of selling the house. The farm and everything. Without *Mamm* there, it's so empty."

His eyes widened. "But it was part of our plan that I would farm it to make a living."

"It was your plan. We never discussed it."

He placed his hand on her shoulders. "Whatever. We can farm anywhere. I just thought you'd want me to take over the farm. Do with the farm whatever you want. But, Gracie, can you give me an answer? I've loved you for so long."

"You have? You've never said it."

"Yes, I have. Gracie, why are you making this so

14

hard? I'll shout it out for all to hear." Silas stood on the log and shouted, "I love Gracie Hershberger with all my heart!"

It echoed back along with 'We knew that'. Had they heard at the house? How embarrassing. Gracie's cheeks burnt crimson.

Silas hopped off the log. "Please, Gracie, say you'll be my bride come next wedding season."

Gracie froze. Her *mamm*'s caution about Silas just wouldn't die. It was seven months before wedding season in November. Could they rekindle their relationship now that she had so much free time? "We can wait until a few weeks before the wedding to decide. How about we court again to see where we are come wedding season?"

He glowered. "If that's what it takes, okay? Why not wait longer? I've already waited for years."

Gracie didn't let his anger distract her, being confident of the path she now embraced.

∞∞∞

Over the next two weeks, word got out that Gracie was going to sell her farm, and her siblings met at Rachel's house. Her brother, Bruce, could attend, but

Luke lived in Pennsylvania and couldn't be there.

"She just wants a new house," Rachel accused. "Poor, Silas. He's wanted that farm forever."

Bruce rose to his six-foot stature. "We're talking about Gracie. She gets to inherit since she's the last to marry."

"And take over the family home!" Rachel near screamed.

This bickering didn't sit well with Teresa, but she had to admit that she was taken aback. Not go into *Mamm* and *Daed*'s house again? Hear all the clocks chime...or cuckoo. "Do either of you want to buy it? I can't imagine the house going to someone, not a Hershberger. It's been in the family for ages."

The room grew silent. Bruce raked his fingers through his blond hair. "I'm already settled at my place. Luke wrote and said he'd never move back to New York, it being so cold.

"I'll write to him and see if he's interested, just in case," Rachel offered. "His *dochder* is so liberal. I died when I saw the colors she wore to *Mamm*'s funeral. Green is a sign of new life and is insulting to wear at such a time. And she plays with Englishers. Maybe we'd be doing Luke a favor by coaxing him to come home."

Teresa groaned. "Alice is a sweet girl."

"They're still hoping for another *kinner*," Bruce said.

"Now, let's focus on the meeting's point. We need to confront Gracie. Tell her she's still in grief and not in her right mind. Of course, the house is empty, but she can fill it with *kinner*."

Teresa had to admit her sister had a point. "I say we ask Gracie to wait for a period of time. She's always so reasonable and–"

"Easy to control?" Bruce pounced. "You two never treated her like she had brains."

"Bruce, that's not true," Teresa said.

"Well, you Rachel, have always been jealous of her and that's why you treat her...not too *gut*."

"Jealous of what?" Rachel snapped. "I have a husband and *kinner* and she's all alone."

"She turned down half the men in the county," Bruce said. "She could have married you know who when she was nineteen, but she said no, and he picked the other *schwester*."

Teresa had to grab a Kleenex to hide her laugh. Rachel screamed at a feverish pitch when she realized her husband had asked Gracie first. Didn't everyone know this? Teresa collected herself and told them both to calm down. "I think Gracie is closest to me, and I'll ask her to wait for a spell. She is acting hasty."

"She told Silas she wouldn't give him an answer to

his marriage proposal until October," Bruce groaned. "The poor guy is like a sick pup. But I have to say I'm proud of Gracie for testing him."

"Testing what?" Rachel asked, rolling her eyes. "Gracie has her nose in the air, acting proud like the Smicksburg Amish."

Bruce put up a hand in protest. "Luke lives there and feels at home. Not a smidgen of pride in him or Abigail. As for Gracie testing Silas, it's a big decision. Obviously, she's not convinced he's right for her."

"She's lucky to get him," Rachel said under her breath.

Teresa shot up a prayer for help. "Please, we're siblings and need to talk sensibly. *Mamm* made it clear the farm belonged to her, since she's the last to marry. But I hoped to have that house myself." She sighed. "But how can I ask William to sell our house that we built together? We must do our best and trust the Lord for the rest."

# Chapter 2

G racie dug holes in a straight row to plant gladiolus bulbs. She had to plan on staying in this empty house for a while. Teresa was right. Their heart-to-heart talk was a soothing balm. She felt looked after by her big sister. And to think that Luke, her twin, was so concerned, he'd let Alice, his little six-year-old, come up from Smicksburg to keep her company. She was overjoyed. Apparently, Alice missed her and near begged to see her more often.

She positioned each bulb correctly in the holes and covered them with dirt. They'll bloom in autumn, during wedding season. Gracie grinned. Did Teresa buy the bulbs with a wedding in mind?

Gracie loved tending her hobby farm, as the fog of depression seemed to ease daily. She liked the pygmy goats, but her hens were her babies. Silas had teased her about rocking a hen on the porch the other night. Well, the hen looked sad. Were others picking on her?

She thought of her sister Rachel and knew all too well the pecking order in families. Maybe that's why she rocked the hen.

A car pulled into the driveway with a realtor's logo on it. A woman with bouncy blonde hair walked over to her. "Hi there, I'm Nancy. Are you the owner of this farm?"

Taking off her gardening gloves, Gracie offered a hand. "I'm Gracie and yes, I own this place."

"Word gets around small towns like lightning, and someone told me you were selling. I'd love to help you."

"*Jah*, word gets around quick, even wrong information. I'm thinking of selling, but I'm waiting until autumn to decide."

"So, you're thinking of selling, though?"

"I won't decide until autumn."

Nancy opened her binder and showed her pictures of comparable houses in the area and their selling prices. Gracie's eyes bugged. She was unaware of the farm's value.

"We have about a hundred acres," Gracie said. "We'd get more than houses without land?"

Nancy's brows rose. "Much more. This farm looks like it's in mint condition and I could sell it in a day."

"A day?" Gracie said with a laugh. "You're very

confident."

"Oh, honey, you don't know. Sometimes when a house goes up for sale, there's a bidding war. People offer over the asking price. I'm thinking you'd get much more than you think."

*This could help my whole family. I could never keep all that money.* "Thank you for stopping by Nancy."

Nancy pressed her business card in Gracie's hand. "You keep this. I will not pressure you. It's not my style. I like informing people about opportune selling moments. It's a sellers' market right now. That allows sellers to obtain the highest amount of money."

"How long will this last?"

"No one knows. Remember the crash in 2008? Houses went for nothing. It was such a shame. But I foresee nothing like that happening between now and autumn. So, you...pray about it."

"Pray about it," Gracie repeated. "I like that. Seems like my prayer list gets longer and longer."

Nancy offered a warm smile and pointed up. "We all need help."

Alice arrived in two weeks and brought sunshine to overcast Western New York. Sunshine to everyone but Silas. He lacked patience for her constant chatter and interference. One evening when they ate popcorn on the porch, Silas put an arm around Gracie and Alice burst into laughter. "Aunt Gracie, how many beaus do you have?"

"Only Silas," Gracie informed.

The man who fixed the fence yesterday kept looking at you. He stared, and we Amish know not to stare, but he stared at you!"

Gracie laughed. "I've known Simon since first grade. We're friends."

"When did you meet Silas?" Alice asked, as if Silas wasn't present.

"First grade," Silas said evenly. "Gracie, you told her we're getting married this fall, *jah*?"

"She didn't tell me anything about getting married to you."

"You've only been here five days," Gracie said, biting back laughter. "Silas and I are praying about getting married, but we have no definite plans yet."

Alice and Silas locked their eyes as if playing chicken. Who would blink first?

"What's wrong with you two?"

Silas mumbled about Smicksburg kids lacking

manners. Alice said New York Amish were too serious. The night fell flat, and Gracie retired early, wanting some time to talk to her niece. Silas was more than eager to leave.

Alice helped gather the popcorn bowls and picked up any that fell on the gray painted porch floor. When they got inside, Alice exhaled. "Aunt Gracie, he's such a grouch."

Gracie motioned for Alice to sit down in the living room. "Alice, I think you made him nervous. He's not used to Amish who are so...talkative."

"I talk too much?"

"Well, I think you know you're only going to be here for three weeks and so you're getting in all that you can say really fast. Am I right?"

Alice nodded. "I think Silas knows I want to spend every minute with you and he's jealous."

"Of you? *Ach,* that's ridiculous. He's a grown man."

Gracie knew she was defending someone who occasionally acted immature. Would he be a good father? Would he sacrifice for his children? "How about we play checkers?"

"I'm not good at it. I want to talk to you about something. *Mamm* thinks I don't know, but she's pregnant again. I'm wondering what it's going to be like when the *boppli* comes. I've had *Mamm* all to myself. Will she have enough love for me?"

"*Ach,* honey. A *Mamm*'s heart grows bigger with each child she has." Gracie didn't know Abigail was pregnant, so she fumbled for words, trying to take in the shock. "You can be a *Mamm*'s helper."

"How do you know my *Mamm*'s heart will grow? Maybe she'll have twins. You and *Daed* are twins, and it runs in the family. What if she has triplets like Louise Graber! I'm best friends with Millie Graber and she barely sees her *mamm* anymore. And washing all those diapers!"

Gracie hugged Alice. She needed to know her favorite aunt would never change in her love for her. "Alice, we'll write like clockwork when you go home. And I'll visit Smicksburg for the first time. Your *daed* comes home so much and we barely travel. It's just me and this big house and I get lonely. And I'm scared."

Alice put her blonde braided head on Gracie's shoulder. "Me, too. Ever since *Oma* died, I'm afraid *Daed* won't come visit up here as much. I came here to spend time with *Oma* since I was three, and I never got homesick."

Gracie tilt her head on Alice's. "That makes you very brave." She took Alice's hand. "Your *Oma* loved you so."

Alice's shoulders shook. I wish *Daed* had come up so I could say goodbye.

Gracie rocked Alice like one of her hens and soon the girl sprang back to life.

∞ ∞ ∞

Alice wanted to visit her Aunt Teresa and play with her cousins, so they took casseroles and desserts over, trying to empty the icebox. Many Amish were still visiting and bringing food, easing the burden of grief. When they arrived at Rachel's large white farmhouse, Alice put a questioning finger to her lip. "Why does everyone have dark blue curtains? They look...sad. We have white ones in Smicksburg. But I like the red barns. We have white barns in Smicksburg."

Holding her close before getting out of the buggy, Gracie whispered, "Is this nervous chatter?"

Alice nodded. "I'm afraid Aunt Rachel will be here."

"Me, too. But, that's our little secret."

"She's so bossy. And I'm wearing green, and she won't like it."

"*Oma* always said it's what's in your heart that counts, and you have love in abundance."

Alice beamed. "We can wear other colors in Smicksburg, even purple, like violets."

"You'd look so pretty in violet," Gracie said. "Let's get this food to your Aunt Teresa."

The two carried baskets into Teresa's house and Teresa soon appeared, opening her arms to Alice, hugging her tight.

"Mmm, Aunt Teresa, you smell like a bakery."

"Sweet girl. Danki. Just made funnel cakes. I bake much better than I cook."

"What's the difference?"

Gracie asked her sister about her children to avoid Alice's nervous chatter.

"They went to the auction with their *daed*."

Alice slumped. "When will they be back?"

"In an hour? But, Alice, I can give you another crochet lesson if you'd like. There's a trick holding the yarn I will teach you. You'll be doing the shell stitch in no time."

Gracie noticed Alice's disinterest in crochet but was impressed that she didn't pout. Teresa accepted the food, saying she hadn't had to cook for weeks, and was glad.

Teresa put a plate of homemade donuts on the table along with some lemonade. "Help yourselves. We can crochet in the living room."

"I'm stuffed, Aunt Teresa," Alice said, patting her stomach.

They sat in the living room. Teresa showed Alice how to lace yarn through her left hand to control tension. "You try making a chain while I work on my doily."

"It's so pretty," Alice gasped. "I'm surprised you're allowed such fancy things in New York."

"*Jah*, we get our creativity out in many ways. *Oma* loved the feel of yarn, saying it calmed her."

Gracie went to the kitchen for more coffee, giving Alice time with her aunt. She loved Teresa's front porch swing and sipped her coffee outside. What she needed was solitude. How she loved Alice, but the chatter grated on her nerves. She inhaled the scents of spring. New life. The scent was always welcome. She pondered what her parents were seeing in heaven and again meditated on Psalm 91. *He that dwelleth in the secret place of the most High shall abide under the shadow of the Almighty. I will say of the Lord, He is my refuge and my fortress: my God; in him will I trust.*

What peace this verse gave her. And Moses wrote this as a song. He led the Israelites through the wilderness, following a pillar of clouds by day. *Mamm* said calm and rest were keys to life. If *Mamm* didn't have a God- given peace that passed understanding, she wouldn't make a big decision. "*Ach, Mamm,* I want to be like you."

The screen door swung open, and Teresa was before her, eyes like buttons. "A million dollars?"

Alice soon appeared. "Wasn't supposed to tell. Oops, I'm sorry if I let it out."

Gracie laughed. "It's okay, Alice. The realtor claims the farm could sell for a million dollars. It's outrageous, but I want my siblings to know, because if I can get that amount, I'd divide it four ways."

Teresa sat next to her, taking her hand. "You have the biggest heart."

"*Nee,* I know too much money would be a temptation," she snickered. "I'd buy...I don't know what, but I know I could, and I need nothing worth that amount. And the money would help my siblings."

"Aunt Rachel, too?" Alice asked, cupping her mouth.

"And Rachel, too," Gracie said.

"But, Gracie, you will not sell until autumn, *jah*?"

"Well, I can't keep a place that would benefit my family. And I could give so much to Christian Aid Ministries. It makes little sense to keep it."

# Chapter 3

Silas picked up Gracie at Teresa's later that day so Alice could play with her cousins. Bursting with excitement, she realized the farm's funds could benefit many. Silas had noticed and asked her if she'd overdosed on sugar.

"*Nee,* but I have *gut* news. Guess how much money I can sell the farm for?"

He scratched his chin. "A couple hundred-thousand dollars?"

"A million!" She gushed. "Can you believe it?"

Silas pulled the buggy over to the side of the dirt road. "So, we'd be millionaires? Yippy!" He ran into the nearby field and threw his hat in the air. "Yes!"

Holding her chest, Gracie heard her *mamm*'s warning. *He loves the farm more than you.* Her throat tightened, as she saw Silas come back to the buggy, a skip in his step.

"Our money woes are over! I could make repairs on

my *daed*'s house and barn. *Ach,* we can help the entire *Gmay*."

He hopped back into the open buggy. "What's wrong?"

"I'm splitting it with my siblings. I'd never keep that amount of money. It's too much."

His eyes grew dark. Too dark. "But we didn't discuss this."

"It's not your house," Gracie retorted.

"But we're getting married, *jah*?"

Gracie squared her shoulders. "How could you keep a million dollars? We're not even allowed to have that amount of money. Our *Ordnung* is against being so rich."

"*Ach,* we wouldn't keep it for ourselves. Like I said, I could help my folks. And what about my siblings? Shouldn't they get some money, too?"

Gracie's heart banged against her ribcage. *Mamm* was right. *He loves the farm or money more than me.* She panted, not wanting to believe it, until she panicked. Anger deep within spilled out like the mighty Niagara. "Take me back to Teresa's."

"*Nee,* we need to talk." He grabbed her wrist. "We're going to hash this out right now."

"You're hurting my arm!"

He grabbed her by the shoulders and shook her.

"After waiting years to marry you, now I have no say-so?"

A dog from a neighboring farm barked and ran to them. Mr. Johnson followed close behind. "Is there a problem here?"

"*Jah*, there is," Gracie pled.

Silas, as charming as ever, said, "It's just a lovers' quarrel, like you English often have."

Mr. Johnson pulled out his cellphone. "We English don't shake our women, buddy. Gracie can get off here and I'll take her home, or I'll contact my pals at the police station."

Gracie leapt from the buggy, trying to keep her legs from shaking. Mr. Johnson held out a hand and she took it.

∞∞∞

It took Gracie a few days to calm down. Having Alice around kept her mind off the dark scene with Silas. Confusion made her mind swing like the pendulum clocks. When the cuckoo birds chirped in the hours, she felt like they were saying 'cuckoo' to her. *Ach*, she needed to get out of this house.

Bruce claimed that all men get angry and there were

no visible injuries on her. When she asked if he ever shook his wife, he said no, but still defended Silas, saying she was trying his patience. Rachel, of course, thought she was being irrational, but she saw pity in Teresa's eyes. She wanted a marriage like Teresa and William enjoyed. Once you step into their house, peace wrapped you like a blanket.

Silas had sent letters every day in her mailbox since she wouldn't let him in the house.

Today, Maryann and Betty were coming over, so she pulled out more food brought over by the Amish community. Again, Maryann said she was on a diet, and Betty brought her a present, an embroidered handkerchief. How appropriate.

When they sat down to crochet, there was an awkward silence. She'd told Alice to stay upstairs and practice her reading so she could have adult conversation.

"We heard what happened, Gracie," Betty said. "It's why I brought the handkerchief."

"That family has a reputation for their quick tempers," Maryann huffed. "Maybe Silas never had a *gut* example."

Gracie's mind was in a fog. A shock of sorts. Gracie expressed that her heart was broken.

"You quarreled over the million dollars?" Betty

asked. "That got around the Amish grapevine faster than lightning. Now, some farmers are thinking of selling and moving to Ohio. They have fewer rules."

Maryann gawked. "Are you serious? *Ach,* money is the root of all evil."

"The love of it," Gracie corrected. "But it says in the Bible something about being poor makes you more tempted to steal and having too much money can make you forget God."

"Absolutely," Maryann said.

Having Alice around made Gracie yearn to have children. Talking to her English neighbor though, made her think the Amish had kids too young. Alexa was in her thirties and was just now starting her family. Confused, she opened up to these dear friends. "The Amish consider me an old *maidel,* but many English have their first child in their thirties. I hear some have them in their forties."

"We have *kinner* until we're old," Maryann informed. "Do you know Emma Miller is pregnant?"

Betty gasped. "She's in her fifties!"

"*Jah,* like Sarah in the Bible, wouldn't you say?" Maryann chuckled. "I guess if it's the *gut* Lord's will he give us *kinner* until our quiver is full."

Emma Miller pregnant? She was her *mamm*'s friend! *Ach,* maybe her Amish upbringing made her thinking skewed. "Do you think the Amish are... narrowminded about women marrying young?"

They looked at her in disbelief. Had it never occurred to them they were mistaken...the whole Amish community.

"You sound like a liberal," Maryann cautioned. "We learn our roles in life from a wee age and we're to be *mamms*."

"It's not written in our *Ordnung*," Gracie dared point out. "Am I supposed to settle for someone I don't love to fit in?"

Betty let her yarn drop in her lap. "Gracie, you've turned down so many men, even your *schwester*'s husband. Are you being too picky? There is no perfect Amish man. He'll be human..."

To replenish cups, Maryann got up and fetched the teapot. "Gracie, I was glad when Rick told me I was the apple of his eye. No one else ever told me that. He was my first and last beau."

"But you were only sixteen. You never gave other men a chance."

Maryann sipped her tea. "I knew from a young age I was no beauty. All the guys in school liked you, Gracie. I was friends with Rick since fifth grade and it led into romance. Friendship first and love follows."

"Have you ever been friends with Silas?" Betty

asked.

"He was the class bully, remember? I was afraid of him. Teased me to no end. When I was thirteen and got acne, he told everyone I had smallpox. My acne got worse because of stress." She tried to concentrate on her crochet. "Maybe that's why my parents never liked Silas or his family."

"They have tempers, like I said," Maryann reminded. "If anyone can mellow Silas, it's you, Gracie. You could be a *gut* influence on him. Smooth out rough edges? I'm a lot smoother since I married Rick. He loved me...to wholeness."

The room grew somber. "You didn't feel whole without Rick?" Betty near whispered.

Maryann concentrated a bit too hard on her crochet. "All my *schwesten* are beauties. I felt like that book, *The Ugly Duckling*." She straightened. "Now I feel like a lovely swan."

"You are!" Gracie said, holding her heart. "You're just as pretty as your *schwestern*. *Ach,* Maryann, I've known you forever and never knew you felt inferior. You are a lovely swan."

Maryann glanced above the scarf she was making. "I know it now," she said with a wink, "and it's Rick's doing."

Could she bring out the best in Silas?

∞∞∞

*Dear Gracie,*

*This is hard. Abigail lost the baby. She wants Alice to come home. Can you come and visit? You have such a way with hurting people.*

*Your twin,*

*Luke*

Gracie covered her mouth in disbelief. Alice sat across the table from her and threw her a puzzled look. "Alice, your *daed* wrote. I'm so sorry, but the *boppli* your *mamm* was carrying wasn't meant to be on this earth. The *boppli* went straight to Jesus."

Alice blinked. "What? I mean, why?"

"God's ways are higher than ours," Gracie said, knowing this might confuse her further. "The *boppli* came too early and—"

"It died?"

Gracie ran around the table to hug Alice. "It was a girl."

Alice clung to Gracie as she screamed out "*Nee!* I didn't mean it!"

"What honey?"

"I wanted it to be just me and *Mamm* in the kitchen and I told God I didn't want a *schwester!*" Alice's slight frame shook with sobs. The spring rain splashed the windows as the wind blew.

Gracie let her sit on her lap and rocked her. "There, there, Alice. God wouldn't answer a prayer he didn't agree with."

"How do you know?"

Still rocking her, Gracie hummed, just like her *mamm* did for her when upset. It calmed her. When Alice's body relaxed, she hugged her tight. Alice, all wrung out, repeated that she prayed the baby would go away, and it did.

"God gives life and, He decides when our lives are over. He never would have answered your prayer, honey. God formed the *boppli* in your *mamm*, but maybe he wanted it to be in heaven with Him. Just think, your *schwester* will never cry or have any sorrow."

Alice leaned into Gracie. "My *schwester* is in heaven already? Do you think she met *Oma*?"

"Maybe *Oma* is holding her right now."

Silence filled the room until the clocks struck eleven and then the chimes and cuckoos echoed off the walls.

"If *Oma* is holding my *schwester*, will she always be a

*boppli*?"

"I think people grow up in heaven. I don't know."

Alice hugged Gracie's neck. "I love you Aunt Gracie."

"I love you, too. And guess what. I'm going home with you to visit awhile. Your *mamm* needs us to cheer her up."

"*Mamm* wants me to go home?"

"*Jah*, she needs her girl," Gracie said.

# Chapter 4

In a couple days, Gracie spoke to Silas before leaving for Smicksburg. To her shock, Silas arrived with his father. They sat on the front porch, enjoying a warm morning, the dew still on the grass.

"Silas tells me you're leaving this house empty for a while?"

"My siblings will take turns living here, along with my older nephews. I need someone to feed my hens and horse."

"I can help," Benjamin Miller said. "I can stay here the whole time you're gone."

Gracie squirmed. Both men studied her, she rose and said she needed to tend to something she forgot about. Once inside, she held her middle. What an odd duck Silas' *daed* was. Stay here? Why? She shot up a prayer for help and put whoopie pies on a plate.

"Here are some goodies," she said. "My family will take care of this old house since they know all its quirks. Old houses have personalities all of their own. The steps have a certain squeak that might scare you, but we've always found comforting. Reminds us of our parents."

"How about I help your family?" He grinned at Gracie. "We're going to be kin come wedding season, j*ah*?"

Darting a glare towards Silas, Gracie told him of their plan to pray and wait until autumn to commit.

Benjamin crossed his arms. "Plain foolish," he grumbled. Plans between you and Silas have been in place for years."

Gracie's parents instilled in her the value of respecting her elders, so she asked Silas to explain.

"It's all Gracie's idea, *Daed*. She's still getting over her *mamm*'s death and just needs time to calm down and be her old self."

Gracie's mouth parted in protest. Silas knew she hadn't accepted him yet. What kind of game was this?

Alice skipped out to the porch. "'All my clothes are packed and ready to go."

"Alice, this is Benjamin, Silas' *daed*," Gracie said.

After Alice threw a smirk to Silas, she bowed a low curtsey to Benjamin.

"Something wrong with your legs?" Benjamin

asked.

"*Nee*, I've been reading about other countries and how they greet each other. Do you know how people in China bow to each other?"

"I'd never bow to anyone but God," Benjamin growled. "You're allowed to read such nonsense in Smicksburg?"

Alice didn't even flinch. "My *mamm* loves to read and so do I. We can read anything moral. Do you know Native Americans greeted each other with a tap of hands. A firm handshake means trouble."

"That's so interesting," Gracie said. "Up here, the Seneca say 'Sengo' to say hello."

Silas frowned. "How do you know?"

"My *daed* did business with customers in Salamanca. You know that."

Again, Silas' penetrating eyes bore through her. Looking away, Gracie was grateful to leave for a while. She told them both to take a whoopie pie in leaving, but Silas asked her to take a walk around the house in private. Taking her hand, he led her off the porch and they turned toward the back orchard. The blossoms on the dwarf apple trees filled the air with a scent that made Gracie miss her *mamm*. They'd picked apples together, peeled, dried, canned, and even pressed them for cider. Her *daed* had planted the apple orchard years ago.

"You want to leave all this?" Silas asked, motioning to the trees. "Time away from this paradise will make you homesick for it."

Out of the corner of her eye, Gracie saw Benjamin examining the horse stalls. "What's he doing?"

"*Ach,* only seeing if any repairs need done."

Benjamin Miller was an odd character, Gracie thought. Through the Amish grapevine, many believed he was given to too much drink. Was his farm in disrepair for that reason? Her mouth grew dry. Is that why he wanted this farm?

"I'll write to you like clockwork, Gracie," Silas said. "And I'll miss you more than you know." He pulled her close and placed a kiss on her lips. "It's going to be *wunderbar* for the two of us to become one." He placed a hand on her prayer *kapp.* "To see your hair."

Baffled, Gracie pulled away. With little experience with men, was she meant to feel... dirty? Was she a total prude?

"What's wrong? Can't a fella give his girl a kiss goodbye and talk about our hopes for a wedding come autumn?"

Her chest tightened. Was love supposed to make you feel this way? Painful? She squeezed Silas' hand as hard as she could. "I'll say goodbye the Native American way."

A look of defeat shadowed Silas' handsome face. "It's your call."

The ride to Smicksburg was magical. Only three hours south, but different terrain. She was excited to see the gardens in Zone 6 as opposed to Zone 5 where she lived. Her brother mentioned they plant gardens on Memorial Day weekend, but in New York, it happened two weeks later.

Alice fell asleep and leaned against Gracie. How she loved this girl. She wanted a girl of her own, if it be the Lord's will. Pulling out a pocket New Testament, she once again turned to Psalms, her favorite book. She read Psalm 1:

*Blessed is the man that walketh not in the counsel of the ungodly, nor standeth in the way of sinners, nor sitteth in the seat of the scornful.*

The image of Benjamin Miller raced through her mind as she stared at 'scornful'. Gracie knew Benjamin didn't want her for his daughter-in-law, since she was a Hershberger. The families never got along since her father, a church deacon, exposed Benjamin's sin. Oddly enough, he never had to repent in front of people. Heat flushed Gracie's cheeks and neck. It wasn't long after this encounter that her *daed* had a heart attack. Benjamin Miller never attended her *daed*'s funeral, his wife saying he was sick.

When her mind took a dark turn, Gracie knew she needed a long rest. Of course it was a coincidence; linking the stress Benjamin brought on the church leadership and her *daed*'s death was preposterous.

She read verse 2:

*But his delight is in the law of the LORD; and in his law doth he meditate day and night.*

Oh, how her twin loved the Bible. Memorizing entire chapters. He delighted in God's Word more than anyone she knew.

Verse 3 read:

*And he shall be like a tree planted by the rivers of water, that bringeth forth his fruit in his season; his leaf also shall not wither; and whatsoever he doeth shall prosper.*

Again, she thought of Luke. He would be a source of

healing for Abigail. It surprised Gracie that her twin said he needed her to help. She grinned. Maybe he missed her. She hoped so.

Luke stomped on his shovel, scooping up black dirt. Abigail wanted a larger kitchen garden. Amish people prefer small kitchen gardens near the kitchen door for easy retrieval of salad ingredients or cooking herbs. His beloved Abigail was rushing forward, eager to make things normal. But when would she cry? When would she show any emotion besides... nothing. Her voice was too flat, and her posture slouched. She was downcast. Gracie was a healing balm to many, and he hoped through her patient nature, she'd aid in Abigail's recovery. Another jump on his shovel and fertile black earth spilled up and out. This farm in the valley was a blessing for them, as the rain washed down and brought essential nutrients, especially silt, for healthy plants.

"You grow in the valley," Granny Weaver had told him yesterday. She'd lost a baby when full term and held her stillborn, the only girl she'd have. Granny said God gave her so many daughters throughout

Smicksburg. God gave her beauty for ashes. *Lord, help my Abigail through this valley!*

A buggy pulled up and his best buddy, Leander, shouted out a greeting. Leander was a mystery to many since he was thirty and never married. If he carried a genetic disorder, surely, he would have confided in him. No, Leander was just too self-conscious of his port wine birth defect on his cheek. It ran close to his ear and covered his high cheekbone and reached under his eye.

"How are you, buddy?"

"Came by to see how you are."

"Fine."

"Right. And that's why you're making an even bigger kitchen garden? It's already twice the size of *Mamm*'s." He took off his straw hat and fanned his auburn hair. "*Mamm* visited Abigail yesterday and asked me to pray for her. She thinks you need to talk to Reed Byler. Maybe he can make an herbal remedy to even out her hormones."

"Doc Pal has been treating her. But I can get another opinion. I'll admit, I love my wife, but I can't wait for Alice to come home. She's sunshine in a bottle, and I could use some. My *schwester* is coming, too, and she's the same. Sweet to her core and fun to have around."

"Your twin?" Leander asked. "Poor thing if you're

identical twins."

Luke shoved his buddy jovially. "You are no...what do the English say...looker, I think." As soon as he said this, he regretted it. "Not that there's anything wrong with you. Just a simple, average guy, like me, *jah*?"

Leander rubbed his birthmark. "If I were English, I could get this thing removed."

"An operation? Medicine? We Amish can do that."

"No, theater makeup. Someone came to *Daed*'s shop and rubbed off her makeup. Her stain was larger, but it was concealed with special makeup. She even wrote how I could buy it."

"No way," Luke groaned. "Hey, God put that mark on you for a reason."

"To mark me as a man not to court?"

"Do you have memory issues? How many girls have you courted? How many still flirt with you? I think you're hiding something deeper."

Leander scoffed. "Like what?"

"Like you're too picky. I've met at least three girls who I thought were marriage material, but you broke up with them all." He bit his lip as if biding for time. Is there any medical issue? Your *schwestern* are married. Have healthy kids."

Leander grew too solemn. His chin quivered. "But my *bruder* isn't. I've told no one...but we have...I can't say."

"You're not sick, are you?"

"I...have...smallpox. Not contagious though. Some think it's acne. Have you ever noticed it?"

Luke would not let his pal get one over on him again. "I wasn't going to talk about my health, but I do have six toes on one foot."

Leander doubled over laughing. "I can't trick you no how."

They kept teasing one another until Luke spilled out his suspicions. Leander rejected girls before they could reject him. "That mark on your face has a mark on your heart. Were you teased when you were young?"

Leander blushed. "Kids will be kids, but when you're told you have sin in your life."

"What? Who said that?"

"Never mind. I need to go back to work. Was going to visit Abigail, but...am not in the mood."

"Buddy, I'm sorry. But faithful are the wounds of a friend. You let the past or other sharp tongues define you. You need to work on that. People compared me to my muscular brother, Bruce, and asked if I have dwarfism."

"But you...outgrew it? Pun intended." An awkward chuckle escaped. "I'll come around later."

Luke inhaled and blew out frustration. When would Leander get over his looks? He said his nose was too big, his lips too full, his hands large and awkward. Luke made a mental note to pray for his friend, the first man his age to befriend him when he moved to Smicksburg.

# Chapter 5

Luke cut though the throng of women in his kitchen to get to his wife. How Abigail loved this knitting circle, but she looked so pale...and agitated. "Danki all for coming over. Our icebox is full and we're grateful." He pat his middle. A diet will be necessary soon."

Janice quipped, "You're as skinny as a rail."

Suzy quickly ran out and brought back a big bag. "Here, Abigail. This is the wool and I'll teach you how to spin tomorrow?"

Appreciative of this knitting circle, half Amish, half English, Luke didn't want to offend them by scooting them out the door, but his wife seemed so haggard. His daughter and *schwester* were due to arrive any minute and, he wanted Abigail to rest. "I appreciate you all coming."

"*Yinz*," Marge corrected with a hoot. Learn Pittsburghese if you'll live here."

Luke grinned and stood tall. "Even after all these years, I still can't accept that word."

Marge slapped him playfully on the arm. "Not everybody says '*Yinz*' anymore. I'm just teasing Luke. Abigail, we'll let you rest for a few days. Let us know when you're up for company. We English can visit just as *gut* as you Amish, *jah*?"

Luke glanced at Granny Weaver from across the room. Such merry eyes, especially with her English friends. Again, Luke gave thanks he was allowed to have trusted English friends in Smicksburg."

They hugged Abigail and told Luke to contact them if she needed anything. He exhaled loudly when they closed the door. "*Ach,* the sound of silence. Honey, are you okay?" He sat next to Abigail, studying her. "Have you been crying?"

She nodded and leaned into him. He embraced her, wanting to protect her from what was plaguing her. Feeling so helpless, not in control, had made him read his Bible more. It gave him a sense that everything would turn out for the good but how long would it take? "It's going to be okay. Do you want Reed Byler's advice? Maybe an herbal tincture would help?"

She pressed a hand to her chest. "There's no remedy for a broken heart." Tears pooled in her dark eyes. "Luke, I'm so sorry I can give only one *kinner*. Most women have so many. Alice won't have a sibling—"

"Listen to me, Abigail Hershberger, I love you. Not for what you can give, but simply for being mine. Half the men were after you before I came to Smicksburg. I'm glad you picked me."

She forced a smile. "You were the one who truly saw me. Who loved me for who I am. I realize you must feel sad. Losing your *mamm* recently and now our *dochder*."

He put a hand to his heart. "Hurts in here, too," he nearly whispered. "My twin was such a *gut* caregiver. She'll be here soon, along with Alice. They'll cheer us up."

She touched his cheek. "They can cheer you up, but not me. I'm too tired to be *gut* company."

"You are a little anemic," Luke said. "Doc Pal said the iron supplements will take time to work."

Again, she leaned her head against his chest. "Luke, I'm sorry I'm so weak."

"Hey, hey, hey. Why all this apologizing?"

"I'm a weak person to not be able to snap out of this. What's wrong with me? Am I crazy?"

"Hush now," Luke soothed. "We lost a *boppli* and, it's okay to cry. And Doc Pal said it would take time for your hormones to balance out."

"I know. But look at this house. It's a mess!"

Her sharp tone startled him. "The house looks clean to me."

"That's because you're a man. Women notice the dust bunnies and things that need wiped down."

Feeling weary, Luke got the broom and swept their honey oak floors. "I'll make sure everything is spick and span."

Abigail burst into a sob. "I'm sorry for yelling at you, Luke. Come sit down again. I need you near."

He rushed to her. "Abigail, I want you to lie down on our bed. Please get some rest."

She nodded in submission, and he scooped her up and carried her upstairs to their bedroom.

∞∞∞

The throng of English and Amish women greeted Gracie as she and Alice arrived. Alice ran to an elderly woman she called 'Granny'. Was this Abigail's *Mamm*? Alice hugged the woman's middle as if for dear life. A tinge of jealousy rippled through Gracie. Alice barely knew her family in New York.

A tall, sinewy, black woman extended a hand. "So, you're Luke's twin? Welcome to Smicksburg. I'm Janice. Can we talk to you a tad before you go inside?"

"*Jah*," Gracie said, confused.

"I'm Deborah Weaver," the elderly woman said. "But many call me Granny. I never had a *dochder* so I adopt them," she said, eyes twinkling. "This is part of our knitting circle."

Each extended a hand and introduced themselves. Granny suggested they sit on the benches near the pond to the right of the house. They walked single file on the stone path and settled into the benches. Alice was near tears, wanting to see her *mamm*, but Granny was firm yet so kind.

"Now, I'm not bossy," Granny started, "but I think we need to let Gracie and Alice know Abigail needs lots of rest. She's not only anemic but grieving her loss. Alice, you'll be *gut* medicine for your *mamm*, but if she would yell at you for no reason at all, don't take it into your tender heart. Sad people can be mad people, understand?"

"When I lost a baby, I was a wreck for at least a month," Marge said. "I regret being pushy. Was I pushy? I just wanted Abigail to snap out of it before Alice came home."

"You were being yourself," Janice quipped. "Abigail knows your spunk and took it well." She paused and glared at Marge's blue streaked hair. "Gracie, not all Englishers are so...colorful, shall we say."

"I'm getting my hair dyed natural looking again. It was just for fun," Marge defended.

Alice let out a laugh. "You look like a My Little Pony."

Gracie didn't know what this was, but imagined it wasn't a plain, brown pony. Concern for her *bruder* rose. "How is Luke? And how can I help him?"

"Give him breaks," Suzy said. "He's worn thin. He's still broken up over losing your *mamm*. I'm sorry for your loss, Gracie. Luke said you were an excellent caregiver."

"Luke is too kind," Gracie said. "I love my family, so I naturally sacrifice to help. You'd all do the same. But any advice?"

Granny's chest rose and fell. "Just sit with him. Let him grieve. No words will take his pain away. We Smicksburg Amish believe in sitting with those who grieve. Do *yinz* do that in New York?"

Puzzled at the question, Gracie blurted they did. How different could Amish be? She eyed the lovely color of Granny's dress. Lavender with a black apron. *Ach, if only we had more color choices.*

"We Baptist believe the same," Janice said, "but sometimes some in our congregation give a one-liner or a scripture verse thinking they've done their share of care. As the pastor's wife, I lead a women's ministry who teach what compassion means. 'Passion' means

suffering. The prefix 'com' means come. Get it. Com…
passion. Come suffer with me. Gracie, I know you
understand somehow."

The pain of being near her *Mamm* as she
deteriorated brought tears to her eyes. "*Jah*, I do. My
*Mamm*'s pain seemed to become my own. Not that I
felt it, but my heart ached seeing her suffer."

"*Ach*, it must still ache," Granny said. "Would you
like to come to our knitting circle while you're here?"

"I, ah, crochet. Can't knit."

"It's so easy," Suzy rushed in to say. Only two
stitches: knit and purl."

"Crochet is better," Marge said evenly. "Suzy, will
you ever admit that crochet is…. more elegant. Lacy."

"You use up too much yarn," Suzy said. "But, if you
buy mine, that's great."

The circle of friends seemed to know this inside joke
and laughter fill the spring air.

Granny pointed to the pond. "I almost forgot. Luke
needs to fish. My husband helped him dig this little
pond. Jeb say his fish call to him so if Luke says that
don't think he's gone daft."

Gracie saw Luke on his porch, slumped over
in defeat. She thanked the women for all the
information but ran to her *bruder*. Alice followed
close behind.

# Chapter 6

T he first few days, Gracie barely saw Abigail. Alice went upstairs to comfort her mother, while Gracie felt useless. The icebox was full and though she had heart to heart talks with her *bruder*, he spent lots of time at his pond. He said the fish were calling.

So, on this gorgeous clear night, Gracie decided she'd go to the knitting circle. As she unhitched the horse, a buggy pulled in, driven by a man so handsome, she had to jerk her eyes from staring. *Please don't come talk to me. I'm not in the mood to talk!*

He yelled over to Luke at the pond, but then headed straight towards her. Gracie reminded herself that she was kind of engaged. Why was she so undone? This man might even be married.

He offered her a hand. "I'm Leander. I bet you're Luke's twin *schwester*."

He was utterly confident, not even a hint of shyness.

"*Jah*, I'm Gracie."

He tipped his straw hat. "Enjoying the spring air?"

"*Jah*. Need to get away. Might take a walk." How awkward! Why was she so *ferhoodled*?

"Need to get away from Luke, I suppose," he said with a hardy laugh. "He can be difficult." His eyes danced, and she knew he was joking. Growing more serious, he asked about Abigail.

"She's not coming out of her room. Wants solitude."

"And *yinz* are giving in to her?"

Gracie scrunched up her lips, and then smiled. "*Ach*, I forgot. *Yinz*. it means you ones."

His smile spread to his chocolate brown eyes. "Abigail can't improve by staying indoors. She needs some fresh air. Some sunshine."

"I agree, but Luke is giving her a few more days. The herbalist man came by with dandelion root that's rich in iron. She's anemic."

His gaze penetrated through her. "Have you taken Luke's buggy out. His horse is real gentle."

"I've never driven on such curvy roads. Need to get used to it."

"I can take you to some of the best overlooks if you're nervous."

"Overlooks? Do you have mountains?"

He motioned towards the towering hill. "These

hills are the foothills of the Appalachian Mountains. Sometimes I just pull over on a dirt road and take them all in. I meditate on the scripture; *my eyes look unto the hills from whence cometh my help.*"

"*My help comes from the Lord, the maker of heaven and earth,*" Gracie finished. "That's one of my favorite passages.

Their eyes locked a bit too long. "Sure, I'd like to see all the best spots in the area. Let me tell my *bruder.*"

Running barefoot, she approached Luke who was grinning to beat the band. Luke despised Silas, and he was playing matchmaker. She'd play his game and get him good.

∞∞∞∞

That night when Gracie returned, she was so refreshed by Leander's company and all the green hills, that did indeed give her strength, she couldn't stop smiling. She pursed her lips to try but failed.

"Did you have a *gut* time?" Leander asked.

"I really did." She wanted to say she felt like she'd known him forever, that he was the best male company she'd ever had, but just sat there like a bumbling idiot, smiling to beat the band.

"Want to go on another ride with me? I feel like we've been friends forever. You're so easy to talk to. And you never stare at…."

"Stare? I don't stare. That's rude. I hope you don't think I was staring at you."

"Lots of people do…"

Baffled, she could only blurt out, "Why?"

"*Ach,* you're only being kind. Want to grab ice cream tomorrow?"

"*Jah*, I would." She covered her mouth in embarrassment. "I'm sorry, I cut you off."

A smile split his handsome face. "Tomorrow works *gut* for me."

"*Jah.* I need to buy a few things. Could you take me to town?"

"Sure thing." He shook her hand. "So nice to meet you, Gracie."

She was blushing and needed a fan. His touch shot through her toes. She tried to speak, but only nodded. "Tomorrow then."

∞ ∞ ∞

Luke was eager to hear how his buddy made out with his sister. Silas Miller didn't deserve Gracie, and he needed to prove it. His sister, Teresa, was collecting information on Silas' whereabouts and in such a short time, such a bad report. He clenched his hands. It would be despicable if someone could prove it.

He heard a buggy pull into the driveway and pulled back the white curtain to see how they interacted. Gracie had a smile like he'd never seen. She'd courted men he approved of, even urging her, but never in his life had he seen such a smile. *Danki, Lord.*

They talked a bit, and then Gracie headed towards the house. Luke hurried to fetch *The Budget* and sat, with the newspaper covering his face. He lowered it nonchalantly and yawned. "Did you have a *gut* time?"

Gracie plopped herself in a chair next to him. "It was awful. He's so vain. He thinks everyone is staring at him." She rolled her eyes. "Such pride is not attractive, if that's why you're asking, Mr. Matchmaker."

Luke's breath caught. "Gracie, you know why people stare at him. That's so heartless."

"Come on, Luke. You've pushed me towards other men, but this one can't work."

"And why is that?" He crossed his arms, fuming. "No one really notices it anymore. I never thought you'd be so...vain."

Gracie's head jerked back, as though struck. "Vain? Me? Luke, what are you talking about?"

Luke shot up and paced. "He is the best person I know. Don't ridicule him just because of a birthmark."

Gracie stood in Luke's way. "What birthmark?"

He growled. "The one on his face?"

"You mean his bruise? It looks like a brush burn. Did he fall?"

Luke took her hands. "*Schwester*, only you wouldn't notice. I'm sorry. I'm protective of my buddy. Can you honestly say you didn't notice the port wine stain on his face?"

Deep in thought, Gracie peered out the window. "The bruise is permanent?"

"*Jah*, it is. A few uninformed folk attribute it to sin."

Gracie sat in a chair. "He's so handsome. I thought you meant people stared at his good looks. *Ach,* Luke, now I understand."

He took the chair next to her. "He's thirty and still not married. Lots of gossip is going around that he carries a genetic disorder, but he doesn't. Some people's tongues wag while their brains are dead."

"And it causes Leander such pain? Like a spark, a tongue can ignite a fire?" Gracie asked.

"Well, we have one here." He grabbed his pipe, filled it with tobacco, and lit it. Taking a puff, he gingerly blew out a smoke ring.

"Well, I'm going to put the fire out, "Gracie pounced.

"I'm new here, and maybe the girls need to notice that someone from the outside see Leander as a very good catch."

Luke choked. "You'd do that?"

"Well, I already agreed to go out on a buggy ride with him tomorrow. I know you set this whole thing up, but I'm surprised at how much I like Leander. I feel like I know him better than some other people I've known since birth."

Luke wanted to grunt out the name, 'Silas', but would keep his own counsel on that matter, until the right time came.

∞ ∞ ∞

Gracie awoke that night, heart racing. She sat up and panted. Why was Benjamin the barn for the evening milking when her *daed* died? They quarreled loud enough to hear from inside the house. This question had lingered in her *Mamm*'s mind.

Slipping out of bed, Gracie sat in the Amish rocker near the window. She opened the window to welcome the fresh spring air and took calm breaths. When she reached for her Bible, she realized her hands were shaking.

She chose to rock and enjoy the sounds of the night. The hoot of a barn owl and the many songs of a mockingbird calmed her, but intrusive thoughts prevailed. Something about Silas' family seemed very dark. Silas had a spooked look in his eyes, as if caught with one finger in the cookie jar, due to their frequent quarrels.

The more time she spent waiting and praying about Silas, the more troubled she became. Her friend, Maryann, said she spotted Silas in English clothes, but she couldn't say for sure it was him. Someone else wrote to Luke agitated with Silas for flirting with a married woman. Gracie dismissed it all as gossip, but Leander seemed as transparent as some of the streams they watched today. And Luke was his best buddy. She had to admit, first impressions could be deceiving, but Leander sure made a good one.

She opened her Bible to one of her favorite verses when anxious.

*Be anxious for nothing but with everything by prayer and supplication, with thanksgiving, let your request be made known to God, and the peace of God, which surpasses understanding, will guard your hearts and minds through Christ Jesus.*

Gracie looked up at the crescent moon. *Lord, I'm*

*asking you again to show me what your will is concerning Silas. I give it to you. Make things clear to my mind. And these memories about the night daed died, I ask you for understanding. All these things troubling me, causing this anxiety, I'm pleading for truth. You made all the beauty I saw today, and everything is in your hands. I trust in you.*

∞ ∞ ∞

*Dear Luke,*

*How are you little bruder? Did Gracie meet your friend? I hope she likes him. I must inform you of something peculiar. William has been staying at the family home at night to keep watch. Now that the rumors got around it could sell for a million, we're taking turns watching it. Between you and me, I wish we used locks and surveillance cameras like the English. Times have changed and we need to be wise.*

*William came home real upset. He mentioned that a person entered the house during the night. It seemed like the man knew exactly what he was looking for. William followed him and the man went into Daed's desk and took out his journal of church business. William realized it was Benjamin Miller. He confronted Benjamin, who claimed he thought the house was empty and was following our bishop's instructions to find Daed's journal. William called him a liar and Benjamin went into a rage. William said he's never seen anything like it. When ordered to leave the house, Benjamin said it would be his house soon, or something like that.*

*William told him he'd be taking the journal over to the bishop, but the bishop was stunned. He never asked for the journal. Benjamin's being watched by the ministers.*

*Luke, I'm afraid for Gracie to come back. Can you ask her to stay longer until we get this straightened out?*

*I'd like to leave you with a laugh. Rachel refuses to believe that her beloved asked Gracie to court all those years ago and is spreading a rumor that he rejected Gracie. Isn't that a hoot?*

*Take care of my dear sister.*

*I'm praying for you and Abigail.*

*Teresa.*

"Aunt Gracie, wake up! Stop crying!"

Gracie panicked and shot straight out of bed as tears ran down her cheeks. "I'm sorry for scaring you."

Alice hugged her aunt's neck. "I have bad dreams sometimes, but I've never cried. I've yelled, though, and that's worse."

Feeling like she was being held down by chains, Gracie reached for the handkerchief that Betty embroidered. "Tell your *daed* I'll be down to help with breakfast right away."

"We already made it. *Daed* and I are *gut* at making eggs and sausage. Are you hungry or do you want to cry some more?"

She cupped Alice's cheeks. "It was just a dream."

Feeling like a sloth, Gracie slipped on her cotton robe and made her way downstairs along with Alice. Her *bruder* could read her, so she headed straight to the coffee, mumbling about how she wasn't a morning person.

"You rise before dawn," he noted. "And I know you've been crying. I sent Alice up to check on you."

Guilt shot through her. She was supposed to be helping Luke with his depressed wife, and here she was, crying so the entire house could hear? "I had a terrible dream." She sat at the table across from Luke. Alice put a plate of food in front of her and she hugged the girl again. "Alice, you're sweeter than..."

"The fudge that Betty Lou makes in town? She won't give her recipe out to no one."

Luke put a hand up. "*Danki* Alice. Can you check on your *mamm*?"

"*Jah*. I love helping people. I'm just like my Aunt Gracie."

As Alice skipped away, Luke's eyes met Gracie's. "Was the dream about *Mamm*?"

Again, tears blurred her vision. "It was about *Daed*. Luke, I had a horrible nightmare about *Daed*! I can't get it out of my mind."

"It was just a dream," he said kindly. "We had little time to grieve *Daed* since *Mamm* got sick soon after. You needed more help with *mamm*, too, and I wish my *schwestern* helped more."

"*Ach,* Teresa helped a lot. Rachel, well, she...bossed and gave out orders."

"Some things never change," he said. "Now, Leander stopped by early this morning to tell me he'd be picking you up around eleven, so you can have lunch...and get fudge from Betty Lou."

Gracie slouched. "Do you think it wise that I get attached since I'm leaving in a week?"

"Are you attached?" he asked.

"*Ach,* I'm just saying I could and I'm still praying about Silas."

Silence filled the room like a mist. Gracie studied her *bruder*. "You don't like Silas, do you? If you did, you wouldn't play matchmaker with another man."

Rubbing the back of his neck, Luke seemed to stall for time. He got more coffee and sipped it for a spell. "Gracie, he's not *gut* enough for you."

"You'd say that because you're my protective *bruder*. But Bruce seems to think it was okay when Silas shook me."

"He what?" Luke said, holding onto the table. "Why?"

"I told him if I could get a million for our parent's house, I'd split it with my siblings."

Luke was red as beets. "And he wants it?"

"He said his *daed* needed to keep better care of his farm."

Luke clenched his fist and hit the table. "Gracie, I'd never shake Abigail. Bruce defends him? What a *ferhoodled* family we have. Bruce just ignores everything. Thank God for Teresa."

"She was the only one upset about it. I want a marriage like she has with William." Gracie reached for Luke's clenched fist. "Luke, I'm not naïve. I see Silas' faults. I've known about his temper since I was a kid. But there's another side of him that you don't know."

He squeezed her hand. "I'm afraid for you. You're too nice."

"Luke, I'm not going to marry anyone until I know for sure it's right. We know that God leads us in peace. We're to let it rule as umpire in our lives."

"Like a baseball umpire?"

"*Jah.* Like that. I'm not settled about Silas now, that's why I'm waiting until wedding season to give him an answer."

Luke's eyes grew round with hope. "So, you're not engaged?"

"*Nee,* I am not. I'll stay single until I meet the one God intended for me."

"Well, *schwester*, I hope you have the best time with Leander today! *Ach,* and I hate to ask, but can you stay longer? I got a letter from Teresa and they're watching the house, taking care of all the animals, and she thinks you need a vacation."

Her heart lifted. "I'd love to stay. I'm not helping much with Abigail. She's barely spoken to me."

Luke's countenance fell. "It pains me to see her in such...pain. Reed Byler has her on some herbs he thinks will help, but it'll take time. You're helping me. It's so *gut* to have you here. Let's watch the stars sometime soon."

The memory of her *daed* pointing out constellations ran through her mind, and she feared she'd cry again, so she only nodded in agreement.

# Chapter 7

G racie waited on the porch for Leander, admiring the pink crabapple tree, dripping with pink blossoms. Abigail could make plenty of crabapple jams, jellies and juices come autumn. Making jelly with Abigail was an appealing thought. Gracie planned to visit to help Abigail in any way. She hoped the herbs helped soon.

The elderly woman from the knitting circle arrived at the house in a buggy. *I never showed up yesterday! She'll think I'm rude.* Gracie ran to the buggy. "I'm so sorry I didn't send word I couldn't make it to your knitting circle...Granny."

"You don't have to come to all of them," Granny said calmly. "Did you stay home and visit with Abigail? *Ach,* I'm worried about her, but cast my cares on the Lord. Take them back though..."

Gracie admired this woman's transparency. "I

didn't stay home with Abigail. I met some new people."

"Who? Anyone I know?"

Again, Gracie tried to curb a smile, but one lit up her face. And she was blushing. "Leander, Luke's best friend."

Granny took a Tupperware container from the buggy seat. "There aren't many young men like Leander. He's Amish to his core. When he went on rumspringa, he near babysat his buddies having a *gut* time. He led many back into the fold. Has a heart of a shepherd, my husband says. Maybe he'll be one of the ministers someday. Knows his Bible, and we Amish preach without fancy notes, as you know." She pressed her hand to her chest. "Have to know it in here. Live it out."

Gracie looped an arm through Granny's as they headed toward the house. "Many call you 'Granny' or the 'wise woman' for good reason. You've given me something to think about already."

"What's that. Come, let's sit on the porch for a spell."

They sat on the porch swing. "Now, what's on your mind, Gracie."

"Too much. I didn't sleep well," she fumbled, but found her voice. "I'm seeing a man in Cherry Creek who's not steady like Leander. How can I help him?"

"Tell me more,"

"Well, Silas has a temper, but he got it from his *daed*. I don't think he's seen a *gut* example of what a man should be."

Granny took her hand. "I don't mean to be blunt, but I am. Saying your beau has a temper from his *daed* is like saying he inherited it. Some think Leander's port wine stain is inherited, but it's not, even though some folks say it is. Leander doesn't make excuses for his behavior to this day. People can be cruel, so Leander relied on the *gut* Lord to overcome the hurt. Made him stronger, in my opinion."

"Were people that mean?"

"Most *kinner* at school got used to it, but one boy bullied him endlessly. Leander always turned the other cheek. Strange notions arose of sin in his life. *Ach,* my Jeb beat it into some thick skulls the medical reason for the stain and it died down, but words can hurt."

Gracie remembered Silas bullying her in grammar

school. "That, ah, bully. Was he one that Leander led to the right path?"

"Nee. He left the Amish. Parents were devastated. Haven't been the same since. *Wunderbar gut* parenting, but their son was a bad apple."

*Bad apple? Was Silas a bad apple?*

"So, this beau of yours needs to repent of anger. It sounds harsh but admitting we're wrong and asking the Lord to help change us, is freedom. I confess every day and it's refreshing. Like taking a daily bath."

Gracie stared into Granny's blue eyes. "You remind me of my *mamm*. She talked like you. Had a heart relationship with…Jesus. Is that okay to say down here? I don't mean to sound like a fanatic."

"Fanatic? To love our Lord?" Granny reminisced. "He's carried me through many a valley." She turned to Gracie. "Come by for tea sometime. Or come to my knitting circle. I need to talk to Abigail."

"She talks to you?" Gracie asked, a tad jealous.

"*Nee*, not really, but I won't let her kick me out of her room," she quipped. "I've known her since a wee one. Has a dash of melancholy, you know. Now she has this postpartum depression along with grief, but we don't go through valleys alone. It's not our way. I'll just sit in her room again."

"What do you do all day?"

Granny winked. "I have my knitting in the buggy. *Ach,* it's a joy to just sit and knit."

Gracie smiled at Granny's spunk. Now she knew why her *bruder* raved over this woman who befriended him when he moved to Smicksburg after falling for Abigail while helping with a barn raising.

∞∞∞

Leander kissed his *Mamm*'s cheek. "Don't worry about me."

"I do. Can't help it. Don't want you getting attached to another fickle girl."

He pat the top of her prayer kapp. "I'm fine. I really didn't think Leah was for me."

"I know you feel rejected again because of that special mark that God gave you at birth. It was his way of say—"

"My *boppli*'s been touched by the hand of God," he finished.

His *mamm* covered her face. "Why aren't you married? Do you need a change? Go out west where your *schwestern* are? Lots of young women going out west. Hezekiah writes that he thinks he found someone."

"*Mamm*, I just met someone new. Luke's *schwester* is one I'm eager to know, but you're afraid of me getting hurt, like I was a *kinner*." He tapped his face. "This port wine stain has made me stronger, not weaker. I believe God's allowed it so I can be the perfect husband and *daed* someday."

"When? Will you marry in your forties or fifties? To a widow with lots of *kinner*?"

Despite her tendency to worry, Leander loved this woman. She fret and fussed over every problem that came her way. Did she need a tonic for her nerves? Maybe he'd talk to Reed Byler. Or his *daed* could talk to the herbalist. His *Mamm* seemed unusually off. "I'm going to be late but cast your care on God. Granny Weaver says that all the time. And pray for Luke. Such a buddy but feeling so low. Tries to hide it…"

"I've noticed that. Is that the real reason his *schwester* came to visit? Twins are close and can sense things."

Leander pondered this. "Gracie may do the trick. She's...*wunderbar*."

"Watch yourself. I don't want to see you hurt."

He kissed her again and headed out to his horse. Once on the road, he had only a few minutes before he arrived at Luke's place. It was how they became fast friends. *Lord, help Luke. He hides his pain. I ask you to build him up. He's lost both parents too young. He's tried to be strong, but I fear bitterness is creeping in.*

He sighed. *Help me not to be bitter, too. Leah being afraid our kinner would have a port wine stain was a shock. But I suppose I should thank you that I know that her love was surface deep. Danki for the strength to break it off.*

He noticed Gracie was leaning near Granny Weaver, seeming to soak in her words. She was the area matchmaker. Was she putting in a good word for him?

As Leander pulled into the driveway, Granny rose and went inside, leaving Gracie exclusively for him. *Ach, Lord. I already want to spend the rest of my life with her. Help me slow down. I don't believe in love at first sight, like the English. Am I infatuated with her beauty?* He knew that must be it, so he wouldn't stare at her today like he did yesterday!

∞∞∞

Gracie was thrilled to see Leander, so she ran to him. "*Gut* to see you. I'm ready to go."

"Hop in the buggy," he said rather flatly.

"Having a hard day?"

"*Ach,* I'm fine. Just have some things on my mind. "Where would you like to go first?"

"The yarn shop!" she squealed. "And then get fudge and then lunch?"

"Fudge before lunch?"

"Okay, fudge after lunch." Gracie twiddled with her prayer kapp strings. Leander hadn't looked her in the eye and seemed so distant. So, he wasn't as perfect as she thought. Her smile vanished, and she decided to savor the ride while appreciating the blooming scenery. Many birds were making nests and she enjoyed seeing them with straw, sticks or whatnot in their beaks, busy making a home for a family. She sighed. What she wanted.

"So, how is Luke?" he asked.

"Luke? He's fine. I don't know if a heart can heal fast. He's missing my *mamm* and his *boppli*."

Leander narrowed his eyes. "He's mighty worried about something."

Gracie blew out a sigh. "He's concerned about me, I suppose. Doesn't like my beau."

Leander stared at her, confused. "You have a beau? Like a fiancé?"

Gracie smiled inside. *Why was he so shaken? Did he like her?* "Luke never liked him and thinks he's up to no *gut*. I think my *schwester* wrote to Luke and told him things."

He groaned. "Is he not treating you right? I know Luke, and he's protective of his twin in Cherry Creek. He talks about you a lot." He rubbed his chin. "I know there's a man named Silas he near despises."

"That would be my beau. I didn't agree to marry. I'm praying and waiting on God and He'll let me know by wedding season."

"We have weddings all the time here. When is your wedding season?"

"November," she said.

Leander blew out a sigh of relief. "So, you'll have plenty of time to think about it. Luke's such an easy-going guy. What's his issue with Silas?"

"Well, he's got a temper like his *daed*'s. Granny just told me that's an excuse and that he needs to repent and ask the Lord to help him." She cracked a knuckle "I'm sure you know I'll inherit the family farm and I've decided to sell and split the money with all my siblings. Silas was furious about that."

Leander slowed the horse as it ascended a hill. "Can't he make a living? Why get so upset about money?"

Gracie didn't know why. Silas worked with his *daed* on their farm, but it was in such disarray that folks wondered how they made a living. Anxiety bore down on Gracie just thinking about the situation. Her chin quivered and she willed herself to show self-control, but a tiny sob escaped. Leander was finally looking at her. "I'm sorry. Things are a mess back home and I'm sure that's why my twin is so upset."

Leander put a hand on her shoulder. "Gracie, you deserve a man you can depend on. A grown man without childish tantrums. I'm concerned."

She dared look into his dark eyes. "Danki. It's nice to hear."

"How can I help? Talk to Luke and —"

"Just be my friend. He has enough to concern himself about."

"Well, I'm going to make it my mission this week to...take care of you. Take you to some places that you'll love. Do you like flowers?"

She nodded.

"We have many greenhouses, some bigger than the English box stores. How about dogs?"

"What about them," Gracie asked, her heart lightening.

"Let's go see some new pups. My *daed* wants me to look at some Australian Shepherds. We use them on the farm to round up the sheep."

Gracie shook her head. "I apologize for not asking about your profession. You're a shepherd?"

"Just like King David, but we're not allowed to play harps, being Amish.

Somehow, Gracie thought this funny, and she let out a laugh. "Do you sell your wool to yarn companies?"

He pursed his lips. "You know, we can ask the yarn

KAREN ANNA VOGEL

lady today how to do that. It could be a nice side job. With the toughest hill behind us, we'll arrive in no time.

Gracie was always in great anticipation before buying yarn. Her creative juices dripped planning a new project. But she couldn't deny that being with Leander was as comforting as yarn.

84

# Chapter 8

Enthusiasm enveloped Gracie as she entered Suzy's yarn shop. It was tiny, but filled with shelves from ceiling to floor, yarn arranged by color. She searched for Suzy, but only heard dogs barking nearby. This was part of Suzy's house. Did she get the idea of having a shop in the home from the Amish? "I'd love to have a yarn shop like this," she told Leander.

He picked up a hank of yarn. "Lots of wool in this. Not synthetic at all."

Suzy soon appeared, leaning over the top of a Dutch door that led to another room. "How are you, Leander? And Luke's sister. I'm so bad with names, I forgot."

"I'm Gracie, and this shop is adorable," she gushed. "Did you spin all this yarn?"

"Most of it, but I carry yarn from other small yarn shops."

"Do you need wool?" Leander asked. "Gracie gave

me the idea of selling."

Suzy's eyes grew round. "I don't have time to card the wool and wash the wool. I buy it already done."

"Can Leander sell his wool to the place you buy from?"

"Oh, sure. They're always looking for wool or alpaca. Can bring in some extra money. It won't make you rich, but it'll give you some spare change."

"Danki, Suzy. When Gracie's done shopping, can you write down the contact info?"

He is such a gentleman, Gracie thought. He'd seen Amish men either stand outside when their wives went into a craft store or be mighty impatient. Were men different here in Smicksburg? A bright canary yellow yarn caught her eye. *Ach,* it was the same shade as a yellow finch. Why could the birds wear such vivid colors, but she couldn't? So, she searched for muted tones, finding a delightful shade of blue. An accepted color in her church district. If she had a yarn shop, she could sell different colored yarn to the English.

Suzy neared her. "Has Abigail tried to spin that yarn I brought over?"

"*Nee,* she's too tired. I'll encourage her though."

"I don't think she listened when I gave her a lesson. Can I stop over to teach you both?"

"I'd love to learn. The feel of yarn on my fingers

calms me."

"It's better than yoga," Suzy gushed. "The tapping of wooden needles is up there on self-help, too. Good for the nerves."

Gracie grinned. "I'd like to learn how to knit. But I won't be here long. And it seems hard."

"Just two stitches, teachable in a day. Crochet looks complicated to me…and it uses too much yarn."

"Delicate stitches, like a doily, are possible with crochet."

Leander laughed. "My *Mamm*'s on Gracie's side. She's always crocheting dish rags or a doily for a friend."

"How's your *mamm* doing Leander?"

He appeared confused by the question. "She's fine."

"She comes in here, as you know. Looks too pale and well, nervous. Someone bumped into her, it being a tiny store, but she jumped like she'd seen a tiger." Suzy's mouth opened, and then she clamped it shut. "It's not for me to say. But she's at that age…"

Gracie thought it adorable how Leander blushed in realization that Suzy was talking about the change of life. It was actually comical.

"D-Danki, Suzy. I've been worried about *Mamm*, but we Amish don't talk…"

"Talk as much as the English. I'm a chatterbox which doesn't help. I'm sorry if I embarrassed you."

"I'm not embarrassed…"

Suzy playfully slapped his arm. "Sure, you aren't. Gracie, you look around while I write down the contact info for Leander. He's not only a shepherd, but in the yarn business now."

Gracie noticed that when Leander relaxed, his blush disappeared, leaving the port wine stain more distinct. *Makes him more handsome.* She couldn't fathom why any woman would avoid him because of a port wine stain. She savored this day, not dwelling on her upcoming return to Cherry Creek in a few weeks.

∞∞∞

After lunch at the Country Junction, Leander took her to a store that sold fudge. Her mouth watered as the smells of the place tickled her taste buds. She eyed the display of peanut butter, walnut, white chocolate, and more. Leander told her his favorite was white walnut, so she told the lady she wanted to try a taste.

"Leander, I always sell out of white walnut when you come in."

"It's the best. Betty Lou, this is Luke Hershberger's twin, Gracie."

Betty Lou put her hands to her cheeks in

astonishment. "You look like Luke with a prayer kapp on."

She laughed. "I'll take that as a compliment, but Luke is prettier than me. I mean, handsome."

Leander let out a hoot, turning heads in the store. Gracie noticed a young Amish woman glaring at Leander and then at her. Women could sense jealousy, so she told Betty Lou how Leander was the sweetest Amish man she'd met. Handsome to beat the band, too. She squeezed his forearm, admiring his muscles.

She glanced at the girl whose face was crimson red, her eyes misty. She wanted the local girls to see Leander's worth, but perhaps this girl already knew and felt hurt. After Leander ordered a half-pound of fudge, they left the store.

Leander seemed annoyed or nervous.

"I'm sorry, Leander. I was so loud. Did I embarrass you?"

As they walked toward the buggy, he became a mute.

"That girl back there seemed upset. Are you courting her? Did I ruin something?"

He gestured for her to join him in the buggy. "*Jah*, you embarrassed me. I don't need pity."

"Pity? I don't pity you."

"Gracie, everyone in town is used to my birthmark. It seemed like you were trying to get them to accept me."

Feeling *ferhoddled*, she had to confess. "That Amish girl in there was glaring at us. I didn't like it, so I blurted out what I did."

Leander straightened and motioned for the horse to go. "I broke up with her. We only courted a few months. Luke doesn't even know."

Gracie slapped her forehead. "*Ach,* she thought you already found someone else. I'm so sorry."

A crooked grin slipped across his face. "I'm not. She was shallow."

"How so?"

"Well, she kept asking questions about if my port wine stain could be inherited. I told her my *opa* has one on his head, but he hides it with his hat. The look on her face, one of disgust, made me call it quits."

"Well, I don't get it. Do you know I didn't even notice your stain when I met you? Ask Luke, he'll tell you. I thought you had a bruise. It's a pity people make such a big deal about it."

Leander looked at her in wonder. "Are you serious?"

"*Jah*, I think it adds character to your face."

Their eyes met, leading to a natural inclination to sit side by side. Leander put an arm around Gracie and her fingers interlaced with his. "Gracie, I can't believe it. You don't see me any differently?"

"*Nee,* I do not."

The horse slowed and Leander led it on to a back dirt road. Gracie felt like she was watching herself in a show. A very happy romance. Silas' scolding face snapped her back to reality. She slid away from Leander. "I'm sorry, but I'm courting someone back home."

He stopped the buggy by an apple orchard, still some white with blossoms. "Listen, I don't know what's going on, but Gracie, I broke up with Leah. Could you do the same with Silas? Luke's not hard on people, but he thinks this Silas guy isn't *gut* for you." He looked away. "Do you love him?"

Gracie knew she didn't love Silas, but her life was in Cherry Creek. Moving away would be too hard. Luke still missed his buddy gang from his school days.

"Leander, I think my *Mamm*'s death has affected me. Each day, I fight for joy, avoiding the falling into the sloth of despond. You are so kind and *gut* company."

"Do you love Silas? That was the question," Leander reminded her.

"Love can grow?"

He took her hands. "Will you write to me when you get back home? Maybe by wedding season you'll know, I mean, think I'm *gut* enough for you. Gracie, it's so weird, but I feel like I know you so well."

His eyes were gushing with pure love. Gracie had to look away. "You know my twin, so maybe that's why you feel like you know me."

He winced in pain. "Gracie, will you at least consider me? Pray and see if I'm the one?"

Gracie desired to embrace him. "My *Mamm* always said she found solace and direction in prayer. *Jah*, I'll pray to see if you're my intended. I can hardly believe I'm saying this, but I feel...close to you."

∞∞∞

That night, Gracie wrote a few letters by candlelight.
*Dear Silas,*

*I hope you're having a good time planting your garden. Is your Daed and Mamm planning a big one? I know how much your mamm hates to put up, but Mamm and I loved doing it together. Maybe come fall I can help her.*

*Silas, I talked to a woman who is considered very wise. She said your anger doesn't come from your daed. I'm sorry, this is hard to express. I'm not perfect by any means, but when I fall short, I repent and ask for forgiveness. And then I turn from my vice and ask God for the strength. Do you remember in seventh grade when I put on the pounds. I was eating so many sweets, I got addicted. I snuck sweets upstairs, a place Mamm forbid food. Can attract mice to the upstairs. Anyhow, I did sneak it, and ate to my heart's delight. What I'm trying to say is that I confessed to gluttony. Over time, God took my cravings away.*

*I'm asking you to repent of your anger. The Bible says to put off anger in Colossians 3. Anger, rage, malice, slander. We're tempted to do all those things. We're to turn from them, repent, and ask God to help us overcome our faults.*

*I thought you had a temper because your dad does. I'm telling you this because we're looking towards marriage, and I can't have a husband with such a temper.*

*I say this in love. Again, I know I'm not perfect. Let me know any faults you see in me.*

*Love,*

*Gracie*

∞∞∞

*Dear Maryann,*

*Pass this circle letter on to Betty, and then back to me. I need advice.*

*I'll be staying here a couple weeks longer since Luke and Abigail need me, and I'm going to take yarn spinning classes. The owner of a yarn shop in town wants Abigail to try spinning, but Abigail rarely leaves her bed. Pray for her. She's anemic or depressed. Luke, too. Too much loss in such little time.*

*I met a man named Leander and we're becoming close. Don't tell anyone, but I don't miss Silas and desire to see Leander more. Maybe this is the sign that Silas isn't right for me.*

*Send me news from our Gmay. I know there's always something to pass along the Amish grapevine.*

*Your friend,*

*Gracie*

# Chapter 9

At dusk that night, Gracie and Luke swung on the porch swing, reminiscing about childhood days. Alice had a friend over and they caught fireflies, darting across the front yard squealing that they'd seen another one. Luke went out to help them capture the poor critters for a spell and Gracie watched him. She didn't realize how much she'd missed him until this visit. Seeing him so infrequently was insufficient. And Luke saying she was good medicine to him shot warmth straight though her. Gracie felt more at home around Luke, too, since her *Mamm* passed.

She gazed at the sunset, ginger hues splashing across the sky. To her shock, an enormous bird swooped down and landed in a tree across the road. "Luke, what kind of bird is that?"

"That's a Golden Eagle," Alice informed. "I think she has babies in the nest."

"*Jah*," Luke said. "We've seen baby eaglets trying to

fly. The mother bird has to push them out."

"*Jah*, and one time I thought one would fall out and die, but the *Mamm* eagle flew under it, and gave it a lesson."

"Couldn't the mother eagle let her baby land on her? Couldn't she catch her?"

Luke shook his head. "They're too heavy by the time they're ready to fly. She can only fly under it. I don't know if she would break a fall, but it would hurt. Like I said, the eaglets are heavy."

"It must make the mother eagle nervous." Gracie knew she'd be getting binoculars out and trying to catch a glimpse of the majestic bird. She'd never seen an eagle in the wild.

"We have forty-some types of birds on our property," Luke said as he stood near his *schwester*. "Abigail keeps a journal of their behaviors and such. I think she even names them."

"She should be outside with us, Luke. Fresh air, nature, it's all *gut* for the soul."

Luke put his hand on Gracie's shoulder. "I know. Maybe tomorrow."

A lantern-lit buggy approached and pulled into the driveway. Gracie knew it was Leander. Maybe he came to see Luke. She took deep breaths, willing herself to calm down. Desire toward Leander was growing as fast as a barn fire.

He carried a bundle in his brawny arms and Gracie made out that it was a dog. "Hello. What mischief are *Yinz* up to tonight?"

Luke guffawed. "You're the one carrying a dog. Can't it walk?"

"*Ach,* she's a shy one around strangers."

Gracie recognized the dog. "Did you buy one of the Australian Shepherds we saw today?" She bent down and started to give the dog a rubdown. "You're not a shy one, are you?" The dog's tail whacked back and forth. "There you go. You feel at home now?"

"He is home, if you want him," Leander said tenderly. "I went back and talked to Mose and he knew you loved the dog."

"You bought it for Gracie?" Luke asked, a lilt in his tone.

"*Jah,* I did. Gracie said she wanted to walk the country road and I thought she needed a dog to protect her."

Gracie blinked in disbelief. Leander remembered everything she said. "*Ach,* that's so nice of you but I wasn't hinting that I wanted a dog." Luke slapped Leander on the back and Gracie had a suspicion that they'd planned this.

"It will have to be Luke's dog. I'm leaving in a couple

weeks."

"You need a dog in Cherry Creek for your protection," Leander said gravely. "That dog really took to you and I know he'll protect you."

Now Luke seemed surprised. "Protect her from what? Cherry Creek is a peaceful place."

Leander crossed his arms. "Against anyone who makes Gracie nervous. Anyone who shakes her..."

"You mean Silas," Alice said. "*Jah*, Aunt Gracie, I want you to have this dog. Silas gives me the creeps."

Alarm bells rang in Gracie's mind. Did Luke know something she didn't? Was she so naïve to even go anywhere with Silas after his temper tantrum? Deep down, she had a notion she'd be avoiding Silas when she got home, and he might not like it. Perhaps she truly needed the dog, and Leander was aware of it.

That he cared for her safety made her yearn to run into his arm and say thank you, but she only smiled to thank him. "What's his name?"

"Shepherd," Leander said with a wink. "Can't forget that name when you go home."

Alice giggled. "Leander's a shepherd."

Gracie's cheeks were burning, and she was relieved it was almost dark. "Do I have to keep that name?"

"*Jah*, you do. So you don't forget the good shepherd."

"Gracie won't forget God," Luke said, slapping

Leander again. "What's the matter with you."

"Gracie knows my meaning, don't you Gracie?"

"*Jah*, I do, and I won't forget." On impulse, she approached Leander and kissed his cheek. "I'll remember."

∞ ∞ ∞

*Dear Luke,*

*How are you? I hope the pain of losing Mamm and a boppli has eased a tad. How is Abigail?*

*How is Gracie getting along with Leander? I remember meeting that sweet man and I admit his port wine stain took me back. It's a shame a handsome man has a birthmark. Only our Gracie wouldn't notice.*

*Silas is in a hot temper. He wants Gracie to come home. He has no claim on her, so I don't know why he stopped by today asking so many questions. Luke, he scares me. He asked about the house's sale and assumed he would get the money. I'm glad Gracie is staying with you for another week.*

*William's getting attached to the house. I'm thrilled but how can I afford a house worth a million dollars? It's not fair to Gracie to give her less. Maybe the housing market will drop like in 2008, and we could afford it.*

*Well, keep everything I've said under your straw hat.*
*Love you,*
*Teresa*

∞∞∞

Leander rubbed his sweaty palms together when he introduced Gracie to his parents, Boaz and Ruth. He had to explain a few times that they weren't nicknames, but their real names, just like the popular couple in the Bible.

"It's so *gut* to meet you," Gracie said while shaking their hands. "I'm excited to see a lamb be born."

"And it's nice to show you, Gracie," Boaz said. Leander glanced at his *mamm* who kept her distance. Well, she loved him and was afraid he'd get hurt. After all, Gracie would be leaving in a week.

"And we have you to thank for the extra money coming in," Boaz continued. "We contacted that company that buys wool." He whistled. "Need funds for llama expansion, despite my wife's fear."

"I'm not afraid of llamas. Alpacas are smaller and… pet-like."

"*Mamm*, you don't even believe in pets," Leander jested.

"Not in the house like the Weavers. Dogs in the house. Whoever heard of such things?"

Gracie slowly raised a hand. "Luke's letting me keep Shepherd in my room with me at night."

"Now, why's that?" Ruth asked.

Gracie's face pinched. "I've been having nightmares about my *daed's* death. Sometimes my *Mamm*, too."

"*Ach*, we're sorry for your loss," Boaz comforted, "but they're with the Lord. It's us who are suffering *Jah*?"

Gracie eyes misted. "*Jah*, that's for sure. I need *Mamm's* advice and well, she's not around. Granny Weaver is wise and is answering lots of questions."

Ruth rolled her eyes. "She's not the only wise woman in town."

Embarrassed by his *Mamm's* behavior, Leander suggested they head to the barn. Gracie surprised him by asking Ruth if she had any advice to give. She described her house's worth and disapproval of some.

"Stay for tea a bit," Ruth said, as she tried to suppress a smile. "Chamomile is *gut* for the nerves."

"It'll put her to sleep," Boaz chuckled. "How about another cup of coffee? We always keep some hot."

"I'd like that," Gracie said.

They sat around the table, munching on oatmeal raisin cookies and sipping coffee.

"Well, Gracie, I hold to the scripture. Money is the root of all evil."

"The love of money is the root of all evil," Gracie said timidly.

"Who doesn't love money?" Boaz blurted.

Gracie laughed. "That's true. Our *Gmay* doesn't even allow us to have too much money. I'd be giving it away to family and friends and some charities like Christian Aid in Berlin, Ohio."

Ruth's face softened. "Now, I think that shows your true heart. You like to help people?"

She flushed. "Well, *jah*, I do."

"She took care of her *Mamm* for half a year all by herself," Leander brought up. "She has family nearby, but she couldn't leave her *Mamm*'s care to others."

"I have siblings. Teresa, my *schwester*, visited as often as possible."

"Luke wanted to be there, but driving a buggy to New York isn't possible," Boaz explained. "He'd agonize over it, but I guess his twin convinced him she liked caring for their *Mamm*."

Gracie covered her face. "This is too much praise."

"He had confidence in you," Ruth near gushed. "Why do you want to sell, if you don't mind me asking?"

Gracie frowned. "The thought never crossed my mind until a realtor pointed out its worth. That money could help a lot of people."

Ruth leaned closer to Gracie. "Did your grandparents build it?"

Gracie told them her great-great-grandparents built the homestead.

"So, the house is priceless, don't you think?"

Gracie gripped Ruth's hand. "I found another wise woman. You've given me much to ponder."

Leander hadn't seen his *mamm* attach herself to any girl he'd brought home. All signs pointed to Gracie joining his family. Lord, let it be.

Boaz slapped the table. "We're going to forget about birthing those wee lambs. Let's get out to the barn."

"I'll come along," Ruth said. "Even though I've seen a lamb born a million times, it's still a miracle.

As they came to the barn, Boaz checked the ewe in the birthing stall. "*Ach,* she's ready now!"

He entered the stall, comforting the ewe, rubbing her head. "Now, don't you be afraid. It's natural to be nervous, but it'll be over soon."

Boaz's calming effect on the animal reaffirmed Leander's passion for shepherding sheep. They were gentle, unless two rams butted horns, but that was rare.

"Here it comes," Boaz boomed.

Gracie took Ruth's hand. "I hope she's not in pain"

They watched in astonishment as Boaz gently pulled out the birthing sack, releasing the lamb from the film and setting the black lamb near the mother's face. Another baby arrived quickly, so Leander stepped in to deliver it since the mother couldn't.

"We have twins."

"Let's wait a bit to see if we have triplets," Boaz said, rubbing the wet lamb with straw to remove any remaining fluids.

They gazed at the fatigued ewe, who soon got up and started to lick her baby. Soon she was lovingly caring for her two newborns. Boaz examined them carefully and then announce they had a boy and a girl.

Leander grinned. "Let's name them Gracie and Luke. But, Gracie you're the black sheep."

She didn't seem to hear them, but reverently went near the little black lamb. "How adorable."

Ruth came into the spacious stall. "Birth is a miracle every time."

Gracie put the black lamb by the mother again. "I'll never forget this. My *schwester*, Teresa, always wanted to raise sheep."

Leander felt like they were a family. A farming family that included Gracie. He needed to shake the notion out of his mind, no matter how real it seemed. She'd be leaving and they'd write.

# Chapter 10

Luke could read Gracie like no other, and she was blossoming while around Leander. She withered around Silas. How could he convince his ever-loyal *schwester* that she had no obligation to Silas? He gazed into the oil lamp, the flame always calming him. *Lord, I'm overwhelmed at times, missing Mamm, grieving the loss of our boppli, Abigails failing health, and my schwester's love life. Give me grace to carry this burden.*

He heard a movement upstairs and soon Abigail appeared at the foot of the steps. "Come here, love."

Abigail gingerly came and sat next to Luke. "They all think I'm crazy."

"*Nee,* no one does."

"Well, maybe you will now." She took his hand and placed it on her middle. "I just felt something move. Maybe I didn't have a miscarriage. Granny told me some women bleed after their pregnant."

Concern for Abigail near choked him. Did he push her for another baby too hard? But, he held his hand, hoping to feel something. It might simply be an upset stomach.

"I want Doc Pal to come over tomorrow. I'm still pregnant, Luke. I've read about such things. My body wanted to rest since that's what's best for this *boppli*. Bed rest is what he needs."

"He? Abigail, you know I love you and would never think you're daft, but you did lose a lot of blood."

"That's from the other twin. Luke, I need to see the doctor." She pressed his hand harder into her stomach. "Don't you feel anything? A flutter. That's what it is. A flutter. I constantly had them with Alice."

Again, Luke heard footsteps and Alice ran to them. "*Mamm*, I saw you leave your room. Are you all better?"

Abigail flashed her a smile. "I believe you'll still have a sibling."

Alice searched Luke's eyes, since even at six, she knew this was near impossible. "*Mamm*, the *boppli* went to be with Jesus..."

"I was carrying twins. Lost one but have the other. Twins run in the family."

The bewilderment on Alice's face scared Luke. Was his wife losing her mind? "Alice, I think *Mamm* is really tired."

"Doc Pal will come tomorrow, or we'll go to the hospital for imaging. We should have done that to begin with," Abigail insisted.

Alice's chin quivered as she hugged her *Mamm*. "I hope they can help you."

∞∞∞

After Doc Pal examined Abigail, his blue eyes poured out compassion. "I'm sorry. You are not carrying a baby. There's no heartbeat."

Luke took Abigail's hand, and she wildly challenged the doctor. "I'm a *Mamm*. I know if I have a *boppli*. I've had miscarriages before, but I know I'm carrying him."

Luke extended a hand. "Danki for making a home visit. It was kind of you."

Doc Pal sat on a chair near Abigail's bed. "You're grieving, Abigail, and it can make us believe things that aren't true. You're in the stage called denial. You're denying that you lost a baby. And I know you've wanted another child, but you're still young."

"It was not another miscarriage!" Abigail screamed. "I want to go to the hospital and prove it."

Doc Pal's eyes met Luke's. "I can order a sonogram."

Anger lit in Luke. "*Nee,* I will not have the *Gmay* pay for something that's needless. Abigail, we need to accept what we can't change, *jah*? Our *boppli* is with the Lord."

Abigail clawed at the bed sheets. "I'll pay for it. I'll sell a quilt. I'm still pregnant."

Doc Pal tried to comfort her. "In India, when we lose a baby, she doesn't talk about it because it's associated with shame. Like she did something wrong. It's most prevalent in the country where I come from, but it's a very sad thing. Yet, in this country, funerals are also held by some. Maybe give the baby a name. Consider the child as family, perhaps you'll reunite."

Abigail's eyes misted. "Women in India feel ashamed? Why?"

"I don't know. You know I go to my village once a year and help medically. I'm trying to educate, but some beliefs are hard to break."

Abigail's breathing became labored. "I did something wrong. I lifted the wet laundry to dry, and that's when I started bleeding. *Ach,* Luke, I'm so sorry!"

Luke held her. "It's okay. You're a strong woman. That wouldn't cause a miscarriage would it, Doc?"

"No. Some women get more energy while pregnant and rearrange the furniture in their house. Some even run, do lots of exercises, play tennis, do anything to keep fit. Abigail, you lifting up a laundry basket wouldn't cause a miscarriage."

She clung to Luke and wept, repeating that she was relieved.

∞∞∞

In the coming days, Abigail appeared to come back to life. She got up early, cooked breakfast and cleaned like a busy bee. Gracie felt a mix of relief and sadness as she realized she was no longer needed and should leave. When she broached the topic, Abigail confessed that she shed tears in private, but she had to move forward. Fatigue still plagued her, and Gracie's help would be needed. And Abigail insisted that they take spinning classes from Suzy.

"This town is lots of fun," Gracie chirped. "The houses are closer together."

"*Jah*," Abigail agreed. "Not many have big farms like the ones in Cherry Creek. I think I'd be lonesome if I didn't have near neighbors."

"You have lots of interesting shops. Is that due to the lack of land?" Gracie asked.

"The men here are more open-minded. They're very

entrepreneurial, meaning they get ideas, start shops and make a living using their God given talent."

"So, individual talent is okay?"

"As long as you don't puff yourself up, thinking your better than others. Luke has wood in his veins. He wouldn't be happy farming. *Nee*, it's bent wood rockers, or custom-made furniture. Do you know he has enough orders that folks have to get on a waiting list?"

Gracie considered how much Leander enjoyed being a shepherd. She turned her head, asking Abigail if she wanted more coffee.

"Gracie Hershberger, I saw that smile. What are you thinking about? Opening your own store?"

"I could do that here, *jah*?" *Why this goofy smile? Gracie, show some self-control.*

"Well, it would be a lot of work, but many women supplement their husband's income by starting small businesses. Some make quite a bit." Abigail eyed Gracie when she placed a cup of coffee before her. "But you're not married, yet."

Silas popped into her mind, which made her stomach tighten. "*Nee*, and I don't think they'll be a wedding this November."

Abigail held her cup mid-air. "So, you won't be marrying Silas?"

"Abigail, I don't love him. I've tried, but—"

"Leander won your heart?"

"*Ach,* nee. I've only known him for a few weeks."

"Luke visited for a barn raising and we knew we were meant for each other when he left. Is the same thing happening to you?"

Gracie smiled. How can anyone not like Leander? He's the sweetest, most handsome man I've ever met."

Abigail smiled. "You know your *bruder* was hoping you two would click."

Gracie felt torn. "I told Silas I'd wait until November to see if our relationship grew into love. I need to keep my word. Leander asked me to write, hoping our love grows."

"Our love. You sound like you already love him."

Gracie shook her head. "It could be infatuation. That's not love. I'm on vacation with no responsibilities, so I'm carefree and there's room for love...to grow. Silas has waited for years for me, and it's my obligation to give him a chance."

Abigail arched a brow. "Sounds like an arranged marriage. Did your parents encourage this? Did you make a promise to them?"

"*Nee,* to the contrary. My parents thought Silas and his *daed* are squirrelly. It's like they're hiding something. I don't know. Maybe it's all in my head."

Abigail nodded. "Our minds can confuse us. I really thought I was still carrying a *boppli*, but it was another miscarriage. I needed to face the truth, and Doc Pal was so *gut* explaining it all."

"*Jah*, I need to face the truth about Silas before I move on."

∞∞∞

*Dear Luke,*

*I have bad news. The barn caught fire at Mamm and Daed's house. It's all so strange. Silas saved all of Gracie's chickens and goats, but why was he so near the barn? How did he get there so fast? The barn is being rebuilt by a work crew, but I don't want Gracie to live in that house alone. She can stay with us. I'm afraid, Luke.*

*Now, my biggest confession. I looked through Daed's journal on church affairs. I skipped over it all except when it came to Benjamin. He got money from the church to fix up his house four years ago. Daed noted no progress made. When he had to give an account, he said he got robbed. How could the bishop believe that? Another account says that Benjamin was seen in English clothing in Salamanca. His response was that he was afraid to wear Amish clothes because the Senecas know the Amish are pacifist and won't defend themselves. I rolled my eyes upon reading that. We've had no issues with the Seneca. They're gentle folk.*

*I'm sorry this is so long. As you can tell, I'm upset about the barn and am kicking myself for reading church business. I'll tell William after the barn raising. Please have Gracie stay with you or tell her she can live with us.*

*Much love,*

*Teresa*

# Chapter 11

After Suzy gave a spinning class, Luke asked Gracie if she'd take a walk with him. Gracie brought Shep, saying he was too cooped up in the house. But Gracie wanted Shep because he calmed her nerves. Luke seemed mighty nervous.

They walked the path behind the house and into the woods. Luke pointed out the blue larkspur and cream violet that were prevalent in the area, not common in Cherry Creek. While Gracie preferred the vivid spring wildflowers back home, she allowed Luke to talk about the Smicksburg area.

"Luke, do you ever miss New York spring?" she wondered.

"Well, *Mamm* liked the wild geraniums. I picked them for her..."

They both grew solemn, just the thought of their dear *Mamm* gone to heaven.

"We're so young to have lost both parents," Luke

said. "Especially when we need their advice."

"We have older folks we can talk to, but I know what you mean, no one like *Mamm* and *Daed*."

Luke cleared his throat as they crossed a wooden bridge that went over a small stream. "We've got Teresa and William. I find them wise."

"*Jah*, they are. Luke, what are you trying to tell me? Speak plainly, please."

Luke sighed. "*Ach*, Gracie, Teresa writes to me and there's been some trouble back home. Someone burnt the barn down."

Gracie's heart jumped. "My animals!"

"Silas saved them all."

Gracie hugged her middle. "He said he'd keep an eye on the place. That was *gut* of him."

"The community is having a barn raising now and until they know who set the fire, Teresa wants you to stay with her or stay with me."

"Really? I mean, why? Barns get burnt all the time. Probably some Englisher who has a bone to pick with…I don't know…someone in our family?"

"Gracie, stay with me. *Ach*, I want you to move here, truth be told. You look years younger, and you have a skip in your step. Taking care of *Mamm* was hard on you. If you live with Teresa…"

"Silas will come around? Luke, what is it you have

against him? You're not telling me something."

They reached a fallen tree and Luke motioned for her to have a seat. "Gracie, you're so pure. Always have been. Silas, during his rumspringa was a wild man."

"How wild?"

"I didn't buddy around with him, but word got out that he wasn't shy around the English girls."

Gracie wasn't shocked by this. "It's our way. We get freedom to see if we want to join the church. Experience the world and realize it offers nothing. Silas got baptized, so it's all in the past. We don't look back, *jah*?"

Luke's face grew rigid. "Gracie, there are matters I cannot share with you."

They sat in silence. Robins swooped down to pick up twigs and dried grass to build nests. Tiny black-capped chickadees fluttered through the brush. In the far distance, Gracie saw a mother deer with two spotted fawns. Shep laid his head on Gracie's knee as if being neglected, and she nuzzled his face in hers.

"Luke, I'd like to talk to Granny Weaver. She's older and is called wise. I like Leander's *Mamm*, but I think she'd like for me to stay."

Luke gawked. "Ruth likes you? No kidding?"

"*Jah*, why?"

"She scares away every woman Leander's ever gotten

close to. Mighty overprotective of a grown man, but I suppose it's hard when people pass judgement on the family over the stupid birthmark."

"Leander told me his *opa* has one on his head but covers it with his hat. *Ach,* the Amish are so *ferhoodled* to think it's some kind of sin or something."

"It's not the Amish," Luke defended. "Well, some of them, but when Leander was younger, Englishers accused Ruth of child abuse. Said she was slapping him, leaving a bruise. It got so bad, she never took him to English stores again, only Amish."

"Leander is confident in English stores now," Gracie said.

"He's thirty, Gracie. Not a child anymore. And from what I hear, he went from an ugly duckling to a handsome swan. I know he's caught the eye of some girls, especially Leah Raber."

Gracie rest her chin on her hands. "He broke up with her. Leander said she was shallow. Courted a few months."

"No way! How did you know? He's my friend, not yours," Luke sputtered.

"Well, we had a *gut* talk."

"Sounds mighty personal." He poked her. "It's better if you stay with me for a while."

As much as Gracie wanted to keep her word, her

integrity, she squashed the silly grin that appeared when talking about Leander and agreed to stay in Smicksburg for a while.

∞∞∞

Gracie took the buggy two miles to get to Granny's house. The windy roads which created blind spots unnerved her. Roads in New York went in between mountains, not around rolling hills. Fear tried to take hold, but she inhaled the scent of May, rich in new pines and leaves. An earthy smell that seemed to offer a fragrance to God. This soothed her nerves a tad. She sang a song an Englisher friend taught her while visiting her church during rumspringa.

"You shall go out with joy and be led forth with peace, And the mountains and the hills will break forth before you. There'll be shouts of joy and the trees of the fields Will clap, will clap their hands."

Gracie sang it louder, even tapping her foot to the lively beat. How she felt freer in Smicksburg. Since meeting Leander. Hopefully, Granny could give her some sound advice concerning Silas and now Leander.

Turning onto the dirt road, she made her way to Granny's house. Three white houses close together caught her attention - two farmhouses and a *dawdyhaus*, she presumed. Luke said Granny's house had a wraparound porch, and she soon noticed it. Vines were creeping up the lattice with red rose buds popping out their heads.

Granny stepped out on the porch and waved. Gracie felt a tang of loss, wishing it was her *Mamm* she could go to.

"Come sit on the porch with me," Granny yelled when Gracie was in earshot.

"I'd love that. The morning is so beautiful."

"Sit here and we'll watch the roses. Jeb and I are amazed by our roses' resurrection, after all these years."

Gracie slid next to her. "So, the roses die in the winter?"

Granny chuckled. "Jeb kills them. Well, he prunes them in February, and I fret that he's gone too far. But he cuts back vines that will give room for fresh growth. There's lots to learn from roses."

"My *daed* used to prune our apple trees so much, it left ugly, stumpy branches, but when spring came, blossoms exploded. Well, I miss it all."

Granny took her hand. "You lost your parents so young. I'm sorry. Do you have *grosseldre*?"

"Gone, too. They got married later in life. They lived

in a *dawdyhaus* behind our farm."

"As I age, I appreciate being Amish. Gracie, did you visit for a reason or are you just keeping an old lady company?"

Gracie beamed. "I like talking to you. You're so calm. Tranquil."

"*Ach,* thank Jeb for that. I used to be high-strung, still am sometimes, but Jeb's the steady one. He likes my spunk, though. We call each other leaning posts. We lean on each other."

"That's a beautiful thought," Gracie gushed.

"It's a reality," Granny corrected. "Sometimes I need to lean on Jeb and he's always strong for me, even if he's hurting."

Gracie wanted to bring up Silas and Luke's concerns but felt shame for some reason. Why?

"Come on Gracie, speak up. Mold grows in the darkness, as I tell my girls. Tell me what's troubling you?"

She willed her heart to stop racing. "I'm kind of engaged. His name is Silas and Luke doesn't like him."

"Kind of engaged? You are or you aren't, *jah*?"

"*Jah,* I suppose." Gracie wrung her hands. "This is hard. I told Silas I'd marry him this wedding season, but I needed time to make sure it was God's path for me. Losing my *Mamm* has my emotions like a seesaw."

"How long have you known Silas?"

"Since we were *kinner*. We went to school together."

"So, Luke knows him well, too. Your *bruder* married one of the sweetest women in Smicksburg. I couldn't figure it out at first, it happening so quick, but Abigail just knew Luke was for her. She admired him. Broke Allen's heart, but he's moved on."

"Abigail was courting someone when she met Luke?"

"Engaged to Allen. Luke's arrival for the barn raising was like finding a perfectly fitting glove," she said. "She didn't want to hurt Allen though, but I told her she'd be hurting herself if she didn't give it a time of prayer and fasting. Luke won in the end and Allen met Becky. It all worked out right smooth."

Leander came to her mind. She felt the same. He fit her better than Silas.

"You and Leander seem to be spending more time together. Do you have a story similar to Luke?"

Gracie met Granny's eyes. "How did you know?"

Granny chuckled. "Your *bruder* talks to Jeb and me a lot. He was fuming about a man not *gut* enough for you, and we all thought Leander would be a *gut* match."

Gracie felt tricked. "Is that the reason he asked me to come down?"

"*Ach,* nee. Alice needed to come home and Abigail

needed you. She still does. I see she's looking stronger since she doesn't blame herself for her *boppli*'s death, but she's hurting. You are *gut* medicine for her. Now, tell me. Has Leander spoken to you in an...intimate way?"

"*Jah*, he has. He wants me to pray and see if he's the right one. His *Mamm* likes me, and Luke was shocked."

Granny chuckled. "*Ach*, Ruth treats him like a *boppli*. He's been hurt in life, but we all have our crosses to bear. No one even notices his port wine stain."

Longing to see Leander overwhelmed Gracie. "I didn't even notice it. I thought he had a bruise or burn. Granny, I can't believe he's not married. He's the best Amish man I've met."

Granny screwed up her lips in satisfaction. "My matchmaking abilities have rubbed off on your *bruder*."

Gracie laughed. "Don't tell Luke. He'll get all puffed up. But, Granny, I gave Silas my word that I'd give him a chance."

Granny grew solemn. "You told me he has a temper. Do you think he'll change after you marry?"

Gracie went down memory lane from elementary school days and then on to her teen years. She'd turned down everyone who asked her to wed, all because of Silas. Did she think she could change him?

Responsible for his happiness? "Granny, can a woman bring out the best in a man?"

"Sure, and he can bring out the best in his wife. But, if you marry a pig, you'll always be cleaning up slop."

"What? Is that an Amish proverb?"

"*Nee*, it's something I've observed. Now, Gracie, if you marry Silas, you can nurture him, love him, make him happy, but if he's not a *gut* man, he'll always return to his messy ways. I'm not talking about being tidy, I mean big character flaws. Does Silas have other flaws than having a quick temper?"

Gracie somehow felt defensive. "Silas hasn't had a happy life. His family is *ferhoodled*. His *daed* scares me."

"Do you pity Silas?"

"*Jah*, I do."

"Is that why you're so drawn to him? Gracie, I hear you have the gift of compassion. Compassion means long suffering. Are you willing to live your life suffering alongside Silas? Or do you want a strong man, like Leander, who you can lean on. A *daed* your *kinner* can respect."

Gracie trembled at the realization. "But I'm attached to Silas."

"Silas is familiar to you." Granny put an arm around her. "How about going inside for some tea? I've said things that upset you."

Gracie bit back tears. "You've made me think."

# Chapter 12

T hat night, Gracie and Abigail tried their hand at spinning wool out on the front porch, it being an unusually warm night. The humming of the wheel, the touch of the wool, and the scent of apple blossoms relaxed Gracie. She hoped it did the same for Abigail.

She reflected upon her talk with Granny Weaver and the fear that overtook her while answering some of her questions.

"What's on your mind?" Abigail asked.

"*Ach,* had a talk with Granny Weaver. Her questions gave me much to ponder."

"She's frank for sure. Doesn't beat around the bush, yet gentle."

"*Jah. Mamm* always said God's path leaves you with more questions than answers."

"Luke says that," Abigail said. "I've got my questions for sure, especially why I only have one *kinner.*"

Gracie admired her sister-in-law. Despite her grief, she asked about her well-being. "I'm so sorry Abigail."

"I know. And your company means so much. You may not know it, but keeping Alice occupied for a couple weeks was a *gut* time for Luke and me to spend just enjoying each other. He's the best gift God ever gave me."

"Granny told me you were engaged. Was it hard to break off the engagement?"

"*Jah.* Allen was a lifelong friend. But he loved me. He said he'd give me time to think. So, I did, and I knew I loved Luke. Allen was hurt, of course, but he said he wanted the best for me."

Gracie gawked. "That's unusual. Wasn't he mad?"

"Gracie, we were friends since our schooldays. So, we were *gut* friends first. We were taught that's the foundation for a *gut* marriage. He may have been jealous of Luke, but we took time apart and sought the Lord's guidance."

Gracie shook her head in disbelief. "I'm so afraid to mention Leander to Silas. He'll blow up."

Abigail's pace of spinning sped up. "Was he a *gut* friend to you growing up?"

"Not really. He teased me quite a bit to get my attention."

"And you gave him more attention?"

"*Jah*. I felt sorry for him. He was teased because his farm was a mess. I guess I stick up for the underdog."

Abigail scoffed. "Luke says he plays the victim. Preys on people's sympathies. Gracie, do you think it's your job to keep Silas happy?"

Again, Gracie felt fear creep up her spine. "I bring out the best in him."

"And no one else could? That's a heavy weight to bear."

Gracie cringed. It was a weight. A weight she'd carried for ages. "Many in our *Gmay* say I have the patience and compassion that can make Silas follow the straight and narrow."

Abigail's wheel came to a halt. "Gracie, God gave us free-will. We're free to choose. Look at what a mess Adam and Eve got us into, and they had perfect fellowship with God. Humans were never meant to change others. That's God's job."

"But, you raise your *kinner*. You try to mold them."

Abigail nodded. "*Jah*, we do, but they can still choose their own path."

Gracie recalled a few friends who left the Amish. Despite her efforts, they departed. And they left a hole in her heart. Was she trying to keep Silas in the Amish faith? And why did she care?

∞∞∞

Silas sent a letter the following day.

*Dear Gracie,*

*I haven't written because I don't know what to say. I know I have a temper, but you don't know what it's like living with my daed. Mamm's afraid of him. If I'm nice to her, help her, he calls me a sissy. Calls me a girl. So, I've built a tough exterior, but Gracie you should know by now how much I love you.*

*You asked me to write and tell you about any faults I see in you. Well, sometimes you lack humility. Your schwester, Rachel, agrees. And you think you're superior to others. That's pride. I admit, I showed her your letter and she thought it was too harsh.*

*Also, I never got a letter thanking me for saving your animals from the barn fire. Improve your gratitude.*

*I'll repent of anger if you want me to, but people don't change overnight. When we get married, you'll see how easy going I really am.*

*Love,*

*Silas*

Gracie crumbled up the letter, growled and paced the kitchen floor.

Luke straightened in his chair. "What's wrong? Bad news from home?"

Gracie felt like her head would explode, but she counted to ten and inhaled. "Luke, sometimes I think Rachel hates me."

"What did she say?"

Gracie smoothed out the letter and handed it to Luke. "It's from Silas."

Hurt pierced Gracie's soul. How could Rachel agree with Silas' behavior? She knew he shook her. Didn't she care about her at all?

After reading the letter, Luke raked his fingers through his hair. "I hope our *schwester* didn't help write this. I doubt it. It's so like Silas. Especially the part about being the hero and saving your animals. Ungrateful? Gracie, you're the opposite."

Gracie poured herself another cup of coffee and sat across from Luke. "Are you sure? And what about being proud? Am I proud?"

Luke shook his head. "How many men have proposed to you, including Rachel's husband, and you said no. Rachel has had a bee in her bonnet ever since she found out Jeremiah was fond of you first." He stifled a laugh. "Gracie, you can't see it, but it's jealousy. As for Silas, he never admits to a fault. He's pulling on your sympathy strings, as usual."

The scent of coffee always reminded her of morning talks with *mamm*. "I'm glad I had a *gut* relationship with *mamm*."

"Hey, Teresa loves you. She writes me and is always asking how you are."

"Why doesn't she write to me?"

"*Ach,* she's used to me being out of state."

"Luke, I don't think I can marry Silas, but I'm afraid to tell him. That temper of his—"

"He's a coward," Luke sputtered. "I can live with you at home for a few weeks if you want."

Gracie grabbed Luke's hand. "Would you?"

He squeezed her hands. "You're shaking. I'd never let you go back there alone. The police still have no clues about who burnt the barn down. May never find out."

"I have Shep. He's very protective. Since Leander gave him to me, I've had better dreams."

"We'll figure something out."

To Gracie's shock. Leander came in through the utility door. He lowered his gaze. "I'm sorry if I'm intruding."

"What? Everything's okay," Luke assured. "Come over and have coffee with us."

Gracie tried to act normal, but inside she was turned upside down.

"Did something happen? Abigail okay?"

"*Jah*, she's out with her *schwestern* for *Schwestern* Day," Luke said, his eyes landing on Gracie. '

"Hey, are you okay?" Leander asked Gracie.

He hardly knew her, yet he somehow knew her. "*Ach*, I got a letter that upset me. I have a *schwester* who's giving me grief."

"About not going back to New York soon enough?" Leander asked.

Feeling like she'd pop, Gracie blurted out, "I don't want to talk about it."

Leander sipped his coffee. "That's okay. I was going to see if you wanted to come over and bring Shep so I can train him to herd sheep."

Their eyes locked. "I'd love that. But I don't raise sheep in New York. I have goats."

"Shep can herd up goats."

"You're joking," Luke said with a laugh.

"*Nee*, I am not. Only a well-trained dog can herd goats, but sometimes it needs to be done. When the vet comes, we have to round them up."

"You have goats, too?" Gracie asked.

"A few, but I'd rather have sheep. They're not as stubborn as goats. Anyhow, I can teach Shep, or should I say I can test him. He may have been trained already. He's not a pup."

Luke leaned on his elbow. "Can you teach Shep to be

a watchdog?"

Looking perplexed, Leander informed Shep would by nature protect Gracie. "Why do you ask?"

Luke glanced at Gracie. "There's a guy in New York I want him to...I can't say because I'm a pacifist, but maybe nip him?"

Concern covered Leander's face. "That man you're engaged to?"

"She's going to break it off. He's a real jerk," Luke grumbled.

"Luke, let me speak for myself," Gracie said.

"I will not let her live in New York unless I stay with her. Or another relative back home."

Leander's expression told Gracie much. He really cared for her.

"Well, I hope you're staying for Ascension Day," Leander said. "We always plan something fun that day for *gut* fellowship. Lots of baseball games and good eats. *Mamm*'s already making up her baking list."

"*Ach*, I can help her," Gracie said without thinking. "I mean, she doesn't have a *dochder* nearby and I can help."

Luke rose, a smile splitting his face. "I need to start the chores, but you two can count my family in on it. It's nice having a relative here to celebrate the holiday."

# Chapter 13

Gracie watched in awe as Leander gave commands and the dog obeyed. "Seems like he's already trained."

"I thought he might lose it if he doesn't need to use it."

"Dogs forget? "Gracie said, holding back a grin. Leander wanted to spend time with her, not train the dog. Her heart warmed at the thought.

"I've missed you. It's been a few days. My *daed*'s been laid up a bit. Fell off a ladder while patching a roof leak."

"*Ach,* that's horrible. He could have killed himself."

"Well, never tell *Daed* he can't do something. He fell when he was halfway down. When my *bruder* found out, he said he'd come home. Hezekiah may stay in the area. Said he has a surprise to tell us." Leander put up a finger, signaling Gracie to wait. He ran in through the back door and soon appeared with a picnic basket.

"Hope you're hungry. *Mamm* packed us a feast."

Gracie wanted Ruth to join them outside on this beautiful day, but she desired private time.

He gently grasped her hand. "Fits like a glove. I know, how corny. But, do you mind?"

Gracie stared into his eyes. "Not at all."

They traveled the path, admiring the sheep and their trusting little lambs. When they arrived at the back meadow, Gracie gasped. "So many flowers! Who planted these?"

"My *Mamm* has a green thumb but hates to weed. So, one year for her birthday I got her a box of wildflower seeds and planted them throughout the field. They grew up fast, especially the purple coneflower."

She blinked as if blinded by all the colors. "It's hard to take in. I've never seen a field of flowers. You were sweet to do that for your *mamm*."

"Danki. She deserves it. Works so hard and some days she'll come out here for hours." He pointed to a swing. "That's a hickory bent porch swing I just brought out last week."

Feeling carefree, Gracie could do a cartwheel. She was a *kinner* again, out picking flowers and taking them to her *Mamm*. When they sat near each other on the swing, Gracie believed she'd never felt so content. This is where she belonged. Leander enjoyed being present in the moment and he calmed her.

He took her hand again. "Are you hungry?"

"*Nee,* not really. All I want is to sit and stare at this view.

They sat in silence for a spell. Utter peace consumed her. "I wonder what heaven is like..."

"I imagine your *mamm* is seeing more beauty than this."

"*Jah. Mamm* loved flowers so much." She squeezed Leander's hand. "You are *gut* medicine. Some days I just miss her so."

He leaned towards her. "You can come back here anytime you want." Leander cupped her face. "I won't be pressuring you, but I have hopes that someday you'll live here in Smicksburg and we'll have many happy times right here."

Gracie felt free enough to express herself, so when their lips met, it seemed just right. "I feel like I've known you for so long," she whispered.

"Luke knew Abigail was the one after a month."

"*Jah.* We were surprised."

Their foreheads met and time seemed to dissolve. "I love you," he said.

Gracie's heart melted into a puddle. No one she'd ever courted treated her with such love...respect.... kindness. She never got too close to men since it seemed like all they liked about her was her looks. But Leander seemed to love her through and through.

"You don't mind my port wine stain? For real?" he asked.

Gracie threw her arms around his neck and kissed his birthmark. "*Nee,* not at all."

"I've been kissed by an angel," he whispered. "That's what you are to me."

Their foreheads met again, and Gracie remembered her *mamm* saying she was like an angel. Deep within, she always wanted to be that for her husband and *kinner.*

"Hey, come up for air!"

Startled, they soon saw two Amish teens, laughing as they walked the edge of the meadow.

Leander sighed. "Great. Those two girls run the gossip chain along with their *Mamms.*"

They decided not to worry about the Amish grapevine and enjoyed their lunch, walked the woods and Leander showed her a hummingbird nest. With his hand in hers, she felt...whole. She felt how Eve did with Adam in the garden.

Abigail and Luke were caught up in the gossip mill by the next day. Even Alice heard how much her aunt loved kissing. But Alice was glad that she picked Leander over Silas. Couples kissed at night, after Sunday singings, not in the afternoon when everyone could see. That she was new in town gave folks much to speculate, since they didn't know her character yet.

"So, are you two getting married?" Abigail asked. "Don't need to wait, you know."

"Abigail, I'm so embarrassed. Word's out that I'm a loose girl when we only kissed one time."

"The grapevine has a different story."

"It might seem like more from any angle. He said he loves me, and I believe I love him, too, but it's too fast. It's only been a few months ago that I was tending to *Mamm* and now, I'm in love? I like things steady."

Abigail poured Gracie a cup of mint tea. "Remember my story? I knew Luke was the one, but I needed time for prayer and fasting. Gracie, you need F-A-I-T-H: Forsaking all, I trust him."

"*Mamm* used to say that. *Ach,* Abigail, that's what I need. I need time under the Almighty's shadow."

"He that dwelleth in the secret place of the most High shall abide under the shadow of the Almighty. I will say of the Lord, He is my refuge and my fortress: my God; in him will I trust." Abigail quoted from Psalm 91. "Your *mamm* got me thinking on that Psalm and I've memorized the whole Psalm. Comes in mighty handy when you need comfort."

The two embraced. "I'm so glad we're family," Gracie said. "I feel closer to you than one of my *schwestern*."

Abigail grinned. "And I wonder who that might be?"

Gracie laughed. "I've decided to love her all the more. To be so nasty, she must have experienced pain."

"You do that, but please stay for Ascension Day. I know Luke wants to go up with you for a spell and he loves that holiday so much. It's because he's such a *gut* baseball player."

Abigail was so proud of her husband. She respected him...like she did Leander.

∞∞∞

Gracie was eager to celebrate Ascension Day with Leander and meet his brother. She borrowed a mint dress from Abigail, feeling as fresh as spring. A white apron also made her feel so light, and she twirled around in her room. "Danki, Lord, for this day."

Knocking on the door, Alice sought permission to discuss an important matter. The girl skipped in and plopped herself on the twin bed. "I helped make this quilt. Are you surprised?"

"*Nee*," Gracie said, laughing. "Do you like to quilt?"

"I like being with old women. So many stories. So much gossip. Aunt Gracie, did you only kiss Leander once?"

Feeling her face redden, she looked out the window. "Well, truth be told, we kissed twice. I kissed his port wine stain on his face as well."

"How come?"

"Because it still bothers him deep down. I didn't realize it until he brought it back up. No one believes I don't notice it, but I don't. It pains me to think Leander is self-conscious about it."

"Well, his *bruder* is coming today, you know." Alice put her hands over her eyes. "He's so handsome, I can't stop looking at him."

Gracie sat next to her. "It's okay to find boys attractive." She nudged her. "Maybe you'll marry someone as handsome as Hezekiah."

Alice blushed. "I kind of have a beau now. He's in my grade and I miss him now that school's out. Does that mean I'm in love?"

"That you miss him?"

"*Jah.* Do you miss Silas at all? Or are you happy with Leander?"

Gracie sighed. She hadn't missed Silas once. "Alice,

you make me think. I haven't thought too much of Silas unless I hear from one of my girlfriends."

"What has he done now?" Alice groaned.

Trying to hold back laughter, Gracie pulled the girl close. "You know, Alice, *gut* character is better than anything, even *gut* looks. My girlfriends, Betty and Maryann, have written some things about Silas that are character flaws."

"Why doesn't he fix himself? I don't like him, but I feel sorry for him. His *daed* scared me."

She held on to Silas for so long because of this. His upbringing and family life was pitiful, but like Granny Weaver said, he needs to repent. "Alice, have you ever lied?"

She looked up, deep in thought. "One time I told a fib to my teacher. I felt so horrible and told *Mamm*. She had me apologize to the teacher and then ask God to forgive me. I felt real washed up like clean laundry."

Gracie kissed Alice's bandana. "That's the key to *gut* character. When you feel guilty of some kind of sin, you ask God to forgive you. It says in the Bible that though your sin be as red as crimson, He'll make it white as snow."

"Is crimson red? Because berry stains never come out. *Mamm* and I will pick berries next month and I need to be careful not to sit in a pile of them."

"Why would you sit in a pile of berries?"

"The berries fall off close to the bushes. I didn't see them. Yet, I believe nothing can cleanse the stain."

"Well, God can take the stain of our sin and make it white."

Alice grew quiet and then looked sheepishly at her aunt. "Aunt Gracie, I've got some stains."

"Well, tell God you're sorry and you'll be forgiven. If you've affected someone, tell them and make it right."

Alice's chest rose up and down. "Okay. Aunt Gracie, I'm sorry I hid Silas' letters to you. I thought I was doing you a favor since he's a jerk and Leander isn't."

Shocked, Gracie shot up with hands on her hips, and blurted out, "How could you do that?"

Alice's chin quivered, and then the tears rolled down her cheeks. "I-I'm s-sorry. I don't like him."

Gracie near ran to the window and opened it up to breathe. *Calm yourself, Gracie Hershberger. Alice is learning to tell the truth. She's learning how to be washed as clean as snow.*

She gingerly walked over to Alice. "Come here."

They embraced while Gracie told her she was forgiven.

# Chapter 14

Alice handed over seven letters and Gracie read them all in order. Silas confessed to a church elder that he shook her and asked for forgiveness. Menno Miller was mentoring Silas, saying Silas didn't have a good example of a healthy dad.

With each letter, he signed it, *With much love.*

Most of the letters were local news, but that he again was learning a lot from Menno. But one letter floored Gracie. His *daed* confessed to trying to hide his gambling addiction. It was why he was trying to get her dad's journal of church affairs. Benjamin confessed and feared he caused his friend's death. He'd gone over to ask her *Daed* not to report his habit to the bishop and they quarreled. It was then that her *Daed* had a heart attack.

Gracie held her middle. Did Benjamin upset her *Daed* so much that his abnormal heartbeat made him have a fatal attack?

She read on that because of his gambling, he wanted his son to marry into money. Silas said he didn't care if she was penniless.

Gracie felt numb. How long had Benjamin pressured his son to marry her? And did it affect Silas even if he didn't realize it? He didn't come around much when her *Mamm* was ill. When she needed comfort. Help. By his action, she doubted Silas loved her. He may think he did, but maybe it was expected of him to marry her.

Luke knocked on the open bedroom door. "Alice told me what she did. She'll be disciplined." He entered the room and sat in a chair. "Gracie, were the letters bad?"

Feeling like she had marbles in her mouth, she attempted to speak but stuttered.

"Take it slowly, Gracie."

"Benjamin confessed to gambling. He wanted Silas to marry me for money. Benjamin may have killed *Daed*."

"May have killed *Daed*? Gracie? What do you mean?"

"They quarreled the night *Daed* died. He wanted *Daed*'s journal and his name out of it. *Daed* was going to tell the bishop."

Luke clenched his teeth. "Benjamin's a bad apple. I didn't want you to know, but he broke into the house and tried to take the journal. William was there and took it from him."

"He broke into the house?"

"*Jah.* Thank God Wiliam was there and wouldn't let him take it." He groaned. "What a mess."

"Well, he confessed to his gambling addiction. Lost lots of money in Salamanca at the casino. He's getting help. We have to forgive him, Luke."

He crossed the room and sat near his sister. "Silas wanted the money from the house. How despicable."

Gracie valued Luke's opinion and asked him to go on.

"Gracie, you're twenty-seven. Couldn't you and Silas have gotten married long ago?"

Proposal after proposal ran through Gracie's mind. How many men had she rejected since she turned eighteen? Where was Silas' proposal? She let her mind run down memory lane and came up with nothing. "Have you ever seen Silas court anyone?"

"*Jah*, lots of Englishers during rumspringa. But, he calmed down and got baptized. I think I saw him with Elizabeth Coblenz a few times. They might have been courting."

Jealousy shot through Gracie. Elizabeth Coblenz was too pretty.

"Elizabeth's parents aways struggled financially though," Luke added.

Gracie remembered Elizabeth never being able to run around like she did with friends because there were chores to be done.

"Elizabeth still isn't married," Luke said under his breath.

"You're right. I almost forgot about her. She's in a different *Gmay* so I don't see her much. Do you think Silas still likes her?"

Luke elbowed Gracie. "We're talking like teenagers. I'm surprised that you're upset. Do you really care for Silas?"

She shrugged her shoulders. "Maybe Silas was afraid to ask me, since I turned down quite a few proposals?"

He took her hands. "Gracie, we're going to pray that God reveals things. You need clear direction."

Still dazed, Gracie followed along with Luke as he prayed.

∞ ∞ ∞

Gracie could hardly believe it was only ten o'clock when she left the house for the baseball field. Too many revelations. Too many troublesome thoughts plagued her, but she was determined to celebrate the Lord's ascension into heaven. It was the blessed hope of the faith. She would hope that God would lead her through a puzzling path. As her *Mamm* had said, stay on God's path, even if it leaves you with more questions than answers.

When they arrived at the ball field, Luke reached for his glove, nearly caressing it. Alice teased him he loved his glove like a *boppli*, and Abigail snickered. She patted Luke's back, saying she was proud of being married to the best pitcher in town.

The family seemed back to their happy unit, and Gracie dreaded the thought of leaving. She was not needed anymore. And there was no concern about her going back home since Silas letters revealed genuine change in Benjamin. Gracie would leave her heart in Smicksburg. She missed her friends and family but... she'd miss Leander. They'd write, but it wouldn't be the same.

Gracie thought the baseball game would only gather a few people, but near one-hundred people showed up. They divided into teams and the wives and *kinner* looked on from benches. She scanned the crowd for Leander but didn't see any sign of him or his family.

Luke pitched the first inning and struck out the first two batters. A stout young man knocked the ball out into the woods, getting a home run. Abigail called out, "Keep it up, Luke. Strike the next guy out!"

Gracie gawked in astonishment and Abigail looked at her and laughed. "You've never seen me cheer on my husband?"

"I've never heard you yell," Gracie said, astonished.

"Well, I've always loved baseball and am proud Luke is so *gut* at it."

"Why can't the women play?"

"We'll be setting up lunch during the fifth inning. They'll break for lunch, we'll clean up, and then get ready for the next game, when whole families play. Alice hit a home run last year."

"I'm surprised. Do they pitch slower for women?"

"*Nee,* her *Daed* was pitching," she said with a giggle. "Alice talked about that for weeks. *Ach*, it's so *gut* to be outside." Abigail beamed. "The fresh air, all the People. Well, the winter has passed, the flowers appear on the earth, the time of the singing of the birds is here."

"That's so poetic," Gracie said.

"It's in the Song of Solomon. It tells me that seasons come and go, and everything is in God's hand." She gripped Gracie's hand. "I feel like my grief is gone like the winter. I'll be accepting the things I can't change. If we only have one *Dochder*, it's what the Lord planned."

Gracie squeezed Abigail's hand. "I'm so glad for you. I'm going to miss our chats when I go home."

An Amish man on horseback ran onto the field. He jumped down and soon the men gathered around him. The animated man was describing something chilling. A fire? An accident? Many women ran to hear, and when Gracie heard Leander was taken to the hospital, she felt faint. Everything whirled and she held on to Abigail.

"Are you sure?" Luke asked. "There hasn't been some mistake?"

"Nee. Hezekiah is with the Lord."

"I don't believe it," one girl screamed. "This is a nightmare."

Luke asked everyone to remain calm. He asked all men to take off their hats as they prayed for Leander's recovery.

After the prayer, Gracie's eyes met Luke's and he came to her. "*Ach,* Leander went with the driver to Greensburg to get his brother from the train station. They got hit by a drunk truck driver. Hezekiah was killed instantly, but Leander is badly hurt."

Gracie clawed at Luke. "It's not true. Someone made this up!"

Luke embraced her. "I need to go home. He's my best buddy."

"I'm sorry, Luke," Gracie sobbed. "Of course, he's your best friend. I'm just so afraid of losing him."

∞ ∞ ∞

Storm clouds rolled in that afternoon. Many Amish waited in the Indiana Memorial Hospital. Luke's body wracked with sobs like bellows. Others burst into anger, in disbelief. But they knew their *Ordnung*, the unspoken rule, that Hezekiah was with the Lord and to remain steadfast in their faith.

When Ruth and Boaz came into the massive waiting room, they appeared years older. Gracie wanted to run to Ruth and hug her but Leah, Leander's old beau, beat her to it. They clasped their hands and sat together, as if very close. Boaz rose and gave an update.

"Our boy Leander has been spared. We're grateful. We don't know why God took Hezekiah in his youth, so I'm thinking it's not for us to know. God is in control over all creation...even our dear boy." He paused and wept. A few men stood around him to lend support.

"Leander is in worse shape than we thought," Boaz continued. "He's being transferred by helicopter to Pittsburgh, where he'll get the best care." Again, Boaz broke down and he wept.

The silence that followed was deafening. Gracie

noticed concern and confusion among the People. Luke leaned towards her. "It must be bad. We pay thousands for a flight into Pittsburgh, and we pay in cash."

A medic familiar to the Amish community, Mike Lee, entered the room. "I want to give my condolences to this wonderful community. Losing Hezekiah is unthinkable. Some of you may feel numb, some angry and confused. You'll have days when you think you're over your grief and then it comes again, crashing like ocean waves. This is normal." He cleared his throat and clenched his hands behind his back, gazing at the floor. "Many of you know Eli Hershberger. I took care of him after his buggy accident and look at how well he's doing today. Never, never, never give up hope."

"But he's in a wheelchair," an elderly woman snapped.

Jeb Weaver rose and stood next to Mike. "This is a trusted English friend. We'll heed his advice because it's wise. Now, Leander will leave soon, Mike will look over him like a guardian angel, and we'll cast our care on the Lord, because He cares for us. Please bow your heads for silent prayer."

Heads bowed, but Gracie's mind went blank for her prayer. Sobs shook her and Luke put a steady hand on her back.

Jeb told everyone to stand as they prayed The Lord's Prayer.

Gracie choked on the words, "Thy will be done," but went on as others were sobbing as they prayed, so she was not alone. After the prayer, she was eager to hug Ruth and Boaz, so she got in line. What seemed so odd was that Leah seemed like family. She was still near Ruth, lending support. The girl's eyes were red from crying and appeared distraught. Had she loved Leander? *Ach,* just the thought made Gracie feel shame. They were good friends, and she was as grieved as them all.

When she reached Ruth, she felt her clinging for support. "You never got to meet Hezekiah."

Ruth's sobs escalated and Boaz took her by the elbow, and they dismissed themselves. Leander was leaving and they wanted to be with their son when the helicopter took off.

They walked out of the waiting room, Leah trailing behind them.

Over the next week, the funeral for Hezekiah brought the People from hundreds of miles away,

KAREN ANNA VOGEL

mostly from Millersburg, Ohio, which Gracie learned
the Smicksburg settlement originated. Throughout
the service and graveside burial, Gracie decided she
didn't like the color black anymore. It was a sign of
mourning, but it made her sink into such sadness,
thinking of her *Mamm*'s funeral only months before.

Word was sent today that Leander was out of critical
care and stable. Luke was so anxious he went with
a hired van to Pittsburgh to see Leander or get a
report. Abigail was visiting her sisters and took Alice
along. Gracie wanted time alone. To sit with the new
yarn purchased at SuzyBKnits and crochet a throw for
Leander would be *gut* for her nerves. The alpaca mixed
yarn slid through her fingers and the comfort it gave
soon had her mind calm.

It being a nice day, she took her project outside after
a spell and enjoyed the scent of ploughed ground, as it
was planting time. Luke had taught her the difference
between an adult eagle call and its babies. She could
hear both, so she walked off the covered porch and
arched her neck to watch. Yet, the nest was situated
too high up among the trees. But she could hear them.
A mama and her *boppli*, Gracie pondered. Her mind
wandered back to the day Leander showed her the tiny
hummingbird nest. All creatures, grand and small,
God cared for them all.

Did the Lord see her? Her desire to get married and have *kinner* of her own? She raised a heartfelt prayer for direction and that if it be God's will, Leander would be hers. The image that haunted her was Leah. What was she to Leander?

After an hour of crochet, progress was made. Gracie would work on it and give it to him herself. She straightened. If Leah can visit, so can I.

A car pulled into the driveway. Another tourist stopping by to get directions? So many windy roads dotted with the familiar white house with white curtains peeking out. When a tall dark-haired man got out, she froze. Silas. She felt split in two. Part of her wanted to run inside and hide, the other welcomed him with warmth. She waited to gauge his fickleness.

When he saw her on the porch, his face split into a smile. Eager as a beaver, he paid the driver and then ran to her. "Gracie. You have no idea how much I've missed you."

She couldn't respond in same. "*Gut* to see you, Silas."

He plopped down on the swing next to her. "Man, that driver drove slow. Irked me to no end." He took her hand. "I'm glad you wrote to let me know Alice hid my letters. I thought you were ignoring me, except for the one letter you wrote about my temper. Gracie, I've been a fool, like the Book of Proverbs talks about.

Menno has helped me, especially with my temper."

She studied him. His eyes didn't look as haunted. His demeanor was gentle. "I'm glad for you, Silas."

He pulled the New Testament she had given him out of his pocket. "I'm studying the Gospel of John in the Bible with Menno. Gracie, I've never had Bible learning like what I'm getting. I chew on 'Let not your heart be troubled' and 'I am the vine, you are the branches'. I've white knuckled life since a wee one. *Jah*, I've been anxious since a *kinnner*. But, *Daed* is getting counseling and I see the change. *Mamm*, too."

"Is that why you were such a bully in school? Teased everyone, especially me."

He rubbed the back of his neck. "I took out my anger on someone as sweet as a peach. That you never gave up on me, well, it says a lot about your loyalty and I'm thankful."

Too stunned to speak, Gracie continued to crochet. Her dreams had been so vivid, she wondered if she was in one.

"What are you making?"

"Ah, there was a terrible accident last week. A young man got killed and I'm making this for his *bruder* who survived."

"That's right kind of you." He slid closer to her and wrapped an arm around her. "When are you coming home so we can court?"

Her heart dipped at the thought of leaving. "I need to stick around a bit for Luke. He was close to those who were in the accident. I became close, too, so I want to visit the man in the hospital."

He tilted her chin. "Gracie, is this man married?"

"*Nee,* he is not."

"So, you care for him?"

Fear nearly choked her. Would he explode on her, shake her again if she told the truth? She had to be honest. "I do care for him."

"More than me?"

He seemed different, and she still felt like it was a dream. A splendid dream though. Silas was acting like she'd always hoped. A genuine believer who showed moral character. "I don't know."

He kissed her cheek. "I've been a jerk. I know that. But, Gracie it's more. I never believed in God at all. I played the game. I got baptized, but inside, I felt like an atheist. Now I read my Bible all the time. It's sweeter than honey. Like Psalm 119 says, 'How sweet are thy words unto my taste! yea, sweeter than honey to my mouth!'"

Gracie loved Psalm 119; it praised God's word and how it changed believers. It seems that Menno made sure to mention this to Silas. "You like Psalm 119?"

"I'm memorizing it," he said.

She smiled. "But it's so long. I think it's the longest chapter in the Bible."

His face nearly glowed. "When you've been a starving man and find delicious food, you devour it. My soul has been in such awful shape. Menno says the more I walk with God, now that I believe, I'll be transformed into his likeness."

Gracie eyed him like a bug under a microscope. "You don't talk or act like yourself at all. It's going to take time for me to get used to this."

"But do you like what you see?"

Her years of concern for Silas came pouring out. Her eyes misted. "Silas, I've always prayed for you. *Jah*, I like what I see."

They embraced and to Gracie's shock, Silas cried. "I'm sorry, Gracie. I shook you."

She soothed him. After a spell, she asked him in for sandwiches. Silas confessed that her goodness made him angry. He didn't believe anyone could be so sweet, so he tried her, trying to poke a hole in her to see if she was for real. He understood her better now that he was a believer.

# Chapter 15

I t took Gracie two days to ask Silas to leave. He'd been a real comfort to Luke, it shocked the whole family. The man Luke despised was now respected by them. Gracie admired this new Silas; he was everything she'd prayed for him to be. But what if it was like the seeds planted on stony soil? It sprang up fast but when hard times came, he fell away.

She packed an Igloo cooler full of food for him and the driver and he was off. They promised to write. Silas didn't pressure her to come home. Alice even admitted she liked Silas. 'He's a caterpillar turned into a butterfly', she'd said.

An hour later, Gracie was in a van filled with Smicksburg Amish to visit Leander. She'd crocheted a thick herringbone patterned blanket right in front of Silas and he didn't seem jealous one bit. When he said he was born again, she believed him. He seemed completely different.

Gracie sat next to a very haggard Ruth and Boaz.

They never missed an opportunity to visit their son. She tried to make small talk with them, but they only offered one answer words. Finally, when they were near the hospital, Ruth gripped her hand. "Pray. Boaz and I have decisions to make." She gave her no time to respond but turned and clung onto Boaz.

Jeb Weaver was sitting behind her and patted the seat next to him. "Come. I want to talk to you."

Baffled, Gracie slipped in next to him.

"You may be troubled by what you see. Leander's beaten up. Broke some bones and lots of bruises. Lost lots of blood."

"But, he'll be fine, *jah*?" Gracie panicked.

"Doctors said it'll take time. He's pretty sedated because of pain, but he speaks some. Your *bruder* told you he was in an induced coma due to seizures?"

Gracie's heart sunk. "Luke can't talk about it."

"Well, every day is a new development. What he'll be like after he's recovered is in God's hands."

Wanting answers, Gracie grew impatient. "He'll live, *jah*? Be able to walk? Talk? *Ach,* I wish Luke had said something. No wonder he's so glum."

Jeb's eyes softened. "He's in one of the best medical facilities in the world."

"Does your *Gmay* have the money?" she blurted. "To do as much as possible?"

He nodded. "We're not alone."

Gracie wanted to stomp her foot. "I know God's with us but…"

"I mean the Amish community. Word will get out and we'll have plenty of money to pay in cash, like we always do."

∞∞∞

Gracie stood by Leander's bed, Jeb shooing everyone out of the room. "You have him to yourself," Jeb said with a wink.

Leander's face was swollen, bruised and stitched up. He slept and Gracie took his hand. "Leander? Can you wake up? It's me, Gracie."

His eyes struggled to open, but then slid shut.

"Do you have questions?" the nurse asked.

"*Jah*. What are all these tubes for?"

"Well, he's on a feeding tube since he didn't pass the swallow test yet. And he's on oxygen since he's off the respirator."

"Why can't he swallow?"

"Well, he's had some brain trauma. Strengthening signals to the body for tasks is necessary.

"But, they will strengthen?" Gracie felt hot, sweat

breaking out all over.

"*Jah*," Leander said. "I have sheep."

The nurse whispered for her to keep the conversation going.

"*Jah*, you have sheep and you're their shepherd."

He looked at her. "Leah, help."

Leah? What on earth? "It's me, Gracie."

He frowned. "No, help Leah."

"You want me to help Leah?" Gracie forced herself to ask.

"I can't. I'm a monitor."

Gracie looked to the nurse for help.

"Leander, you've been in a car accident, and we showed you your face. You're not a monster."

"I'm a monitor," he cried out and then sobbed a piercing scream.

Two men rushed in, the nurse calling out orders to sedate him. Leander cried and Gracie just squeezed his hand, telling him he was not a monster. This made him cry all the more.

She waited for a spell until the medicine calmed him down and he fell asleep. Gracie left the blanket she made with the nurse and joined the others in the waiting room, trying to keep her chin from quivering.

∞ ∞ ∞

That night, Gracie asked Luke if they could sit on the front porch for a talk.

"Gracie, maybe you shouldn't visit Leander if it upsets you too much."

"It's not Leander's condition. The doctor assured us that Leander will fully recover, although it will take time."

"Really? That's *gut, jah*?"

"*Jah*, it is. But, Luke, my visit with Leander made me...not trust him. I think he was seeing me and Leah at the same time."

Luke swung a foot onto his knee. "He'd never do such a thing."

Gracie fidgeted with her kapp strings. "Well, he kept asking for me to take care of Leah. Does that make any sense?"

Pulling on his beard, Luke shook his head.

"Why is Leah with Ruth and Boaz as though they were family? Leah took it harder than most that Leander got hurt. She must care for him."

Luke took out his pipe, lit it and blew out a smoke ring. "This is some mystery to me. He's talked about

Leah in the past. Maybe he's confused. Talking about things that aren't happening."

"Or, maybe he realizes he loves Leah now. I think I need to get away," she said, biting back tears.

"*Ach,* Gracie don't cry. Maybe Silas visiting has you all emotional."

"I thought Leander was the perfect man."

"That spot is not deserved by any man. Abigail knows I'm not perfect."

"Luke, you know what I mean. Perfect for me. Haven't felt that way about anyone before. It was like we had a soul bond. This will sound *ferhoodled,* but I felt close to God around him."

Luke puffed another ring of smoke. "Well, I understand that. Abigail and I felt a supernatural bond we couldn't shake. We gave it time, though. Lots of prayer and fasting. Time apart, too. Our emotions told us to get married the first day we met, but we can't trust our emotions on such a big decision."

Gracie pressed a hand to her heart. "That's the best advice I've gotten. Danki, Luke."

"Glad to help."

Contrary to how she felt, Gracie forced herself to say the dreaded words. "I think it's time for me to go home."

Luke frowned. "Do you miss Silas? Care for him?"

"I don't know my mind anymore. But one thing I know is that I miss my friends, my garden, my animals."

His eyes grew tender. "I'll miss you."

"Me, too."

∞ ∞ ∞

The next morning, Granny Weaver arrived with pies. "Nothing like pie for breakfast. It's strawberry pie since they're in season."

Abigail took the basket, opened it, and inhaled. "Danki. They smell delicious."

"They're still warm. Made them this morning. I know it's late for breakfast, but how about a second breakfast, like we have second coffee?"

"It's only the three of us," Abigail said, motioning to Gracie. "Alice and Luke went to visit Ruth and Boaz. Alice made them a card and insisted on delivering it herself."

"She's a sweetheart," Granny gushed. "How are you, Gracie?"

Gracie couldn't resist this woman and rose to embrace her. "I'm okay. Leaving soon."

"*Ach,* for real? You never came to my knitting circle."

Gracie opened her mouth to speak, but nothing came out.

Abigail chuckled. "She's trying to get you to stay here forever. Granny, Gracie has a life in New York."

She dished up three pieces of pie and they sat around the table. "Does anyone want coffee?"

"I do," Granny admitted. "These old bones are tired. I've never traveled so much as I have in the past two weeks. When I get into Pittsburgh, I wonder how a body can stand to live there with all the noise."

"We're country bumpkins, Granny, but some people aren't," Abigail said. "Some wonder what we do so far out in the country."

"We enjoy God's creation is what. Jeb believes humans belong in a garden, just like Adam and Eve. "Now, Gracie, why are you leaving for real?"

Gracie gasped at the woman's frankness. "I miss my...goats."

"Your goats?"

"*Jah*, my goats. And my chickens."

Granny's eyes widened. "*Ach,* how can you miss chickens?"

"Well, I pet them. Hold them. And I want to get my dog used to my place."

Granny dropped the questions while they enjoyed their pie, but once done, she asked Gracie if she'd like to talk. Gracie was eager, so they walked to Luke's pond and sat on a bench.

"Men and fish. What is it with men and fish?" Granny asked. "Do you know Jeb has gone to Lake Erie to ice fish?"

"*Nee*, but I know lots of Amish who do. My *daed* used to take Luke and Bruce."

"So, it wasn't my Jeb who got Luke into fishing. Sounds like you had fine parents. How are you doing with your loss?"

Gracie watched the sun glisten on the pond. "I know they're in heaven, and that takes the sting away. But I miss them."

Granny took Gracie's hand. "I came to talk to you about Leander. Jeb told me you were mighty upset while visiting him. Do you want to talk about it?"

Like a mother hen, Granny seemed to take people under her wings, and the comfort pried her open. "I think Leander loves Leah. That's all he talked about during our quick visit. He told me he broke things off, so I've lost trust."

Granny sighed. "Leander is an honest man. If he told you they broke things off, he broke things off."

"Why is Leah always over at Ruth and Boaz's farm? Like she's family."

"She's a sweet girl. Maybe she wants to help.

Leander's *schwestern* don't live nearby. I was hoping one would stay with Ruth for a while, but they headed back to their homes. I don't fault them. Everyone grieves in their own way."

Gracie stiffened. "When he looked at me, he knew who I was and got really agitated. Called himself a monster and screamed. I don't think he wants me near him, so I don't see any reason to stay."

"Gracie, he's had a head trauma. It's going to take time, but he'll be right as rain again." She squeezed her hand. "Now, my question is, if he came to and explained all to you, would you understand? I'm asking if you love him."

"Granny, I know I do. I can't explain it. It sounds like a schoolgirl crush, but I've met no one I connect with like Leander."

"So, why not stay and visit him. Be a help to Ruth and Boaz?"

"Because I'm too *ferhoodled* in my head. My old beau visited and he's a changed man. He was an atheist and is now what he calls a 'born again' Christian. Amish don't talk like that, but he was a new person. I need to go home and talk to him—"

"So, you're doing what you're accusing Leander of doing. Courting two men."

"What? *Nee,* I was courting Silas and broke it off."

"And now you're giving him a second chance."

Gracie burst into tears. "I'm afraid Leander doesn't care for me at all. Granny, I don't want to be single forever. I want a family and *kinner*. Silas loves me, and he may be my last chance. I need to wake up and smell the coffee, like the English say."

"Marry someone you don't love?" Granny near whispered. "Give it time, Gracie. It would be tough to bear that burden. Marriage is God's greatest gift. Let Him give it to you."

"H-How?"

Granny embraced Gracie. "Stay on the right path."

Gracie recalled her *Mamm* saying that the right path may leave you with more questions than answers. As Granny soothed her, she realized how much she missed her *Mamm*, even her *Oma*. She needed the comfort of things familiar. She needed to go home.

# Chapter 16

**M**emories ran through Gracie's mind as the van pulled into her childhood home. At the empty clothesline, she was a wee one lifting socks so *Mamm* could pin them up. *Daed* would come around from the back of the house, sneak up on them and tickle *Mamm* before he embraced her to plant a kiss on her cheek. *Ach,* such a marriage.

Shep seemed to know he was home. His tail wagged to beat the band. Gracie paid the driver, grabbed her suitcase, and led her dog towards the house. The cooler temperatures in New York, the crisp air, the many pines, welcomed her home. Smicksburg seemed like something from long ago. She was moving on, would get her hands busy. Gardening, making quilts, crocheting, and baking. She'd considered a quilting circle and sell quilts for income.

What an odd position she was in. Amish women lived at home with their parents until they married, but she had no parents. If she never married, a small house would be built on a relative's land. Gracie loved how the elderly were taken care of in a *dawdyhaus*, but she shivered to think she'd be living in one made for an old *maidel*.

Well, no one had mentioned it yet, because they thought she'd be marrying Silas. Maybe she would, so why say anything to the contrary? She'd written to him before she left Luke's so maybe he'd visit tomorrow.

Gracie led Shep by a leash to the back of the house where her goats, chickens, and horse lived in their shelters. She eyed a buggy someone painted shiny black. How nice. Did Bruce do this for her? Despite their differences, she was glad to have siblings. She was determined to get the jaggers out of Rachel somehow. Teresa was a healing balm. And her sister-friends were the best.

She sat on a bench her *Daed* had built around a tree and pet Shep. "I'm glad to have you." Gracie hugged him and any feelings toward Leander were shoved deep down where they belonged. She'd been on vacation in Smicksburg. No responsibilities but free as the eagles that learned to fly. She had to keep moving forward. Put Leander in the past.

Gracie heard the clocks inside chime or cuckoo ten

times. The day was young, and she would have plenty of time to make the house spick and span. Her hands were eager to work, so she let Shep inside and to her utter shock, the house was clean enough to hold a church service. Did the women know she was coming home and surprise her? She walked over to the table where she'd sipped many a cup of coffee with her *Mamm* and noticed a letter.

*Dear Gracie,*

*Welcome home! I'm so glad you're back! Betty and I are getting together tonight. It's a Wednesday when you read this right? Luke called your sister, Teresa, from his phone shanty to theirs. It's a wonder we have answering machines now. So, word spread like lightning our Gracie is home, home, home! I have missed you. We'll be meeting at my house. Wait until you see how big Betty is! I think she's carrying twins.*

*Well, I hope to see you at six o'clock. Enjoy the dinners in your icebox. Your schwestern filled it up. I made the pie.*

*Maryann*

Gracie hugged herself. She was home. And she was missed. How could she ever consider living in Smicksburg?

Buggy wheels rattled, and she looked through the window to see someone. Benjamin? Fear shot up her spine. Did he think she wasn't home? Was he snooping around again?

Her relief came when someone knocked on the door. She welcomed him, forcing a smile.

"Welcome home, Gracie. Everyone in the *Gmay* wants to see you, but I came to say something."

"Do you want coffee?" Gracie asked.

"*Nee*. I'm fine. I need to confess to you all that I've done."

Gracie put her hand up. "I've heard. No need to feel bad. I forgive you."

"Gracie, I've been a wicked man. I've coveted my your *daed*'s..."

Gracie closed her eyes. Please don't say wife!

"I've coveted his lands and houses. My poor wife has suffered much from my gambling, being a drunk, and not giving her the home or man she deserves."

"Why confess to me?"

"Because Silas had a poor example of a *Daed*. I made him lust for this farm. You see, I wanted it. Such a *wunderbar gut* house would be in the family if you two wed. But, no more. I'm working hard. Got a roofing job with the English and bring home a decent income. Silas helped me build veal stalls and an Englisher will bring in the wee cows and we'll keep them for three or four months. So, we're in the farming business, too." He leaned closer. "The English don't want to get their hands dirty, so they have us Amish do it, since we're known for farming." He slapped his knee. "I like hard work. Keeps me out of trouble. Now, Silas is working hard, too. We don't need this farmhouse and land because we're making all kinds of repairs on our own place."

Taken back by this new Benjamin, Gracie could only shake her head in amazement. "That's *wunderbar*. Sounds like too much work."

He lowered his head. "I've had lots of help. Body and soul type thing. Gracie, we have a *Gmay* like no other. Men showed up, helped me do lots of repairs, and the women came and painted the inside of the house a nice mint color. So, I've gotten help in many ways. I was too proud to accept it at first, but the bishop said I lacked humility. Do you forgive me for quarreling with your *daed* the night he died?" His face contorted, and fear was etched on his brow. "I wanted his journal on church affairs and wrestled with him to get it. He fell over and bruised his head. Maybe I killed him. Brought on the heart attack—"

"Stop, Benjamin. You're forgiven. Don't hold on to such guilt." Gracie, moved with compassion, took Benjamin's hand. "We move forward, *jah*? All is well, Benjamin."

"*Danki*," he said, voice quavering. "One more

confession and we'll put everything in the past." He bowed his head as if in prayer. "The barn fire was my fault. I left a lantern on while visiting your goats. I know I wasn't supposed to step foot on your property, but those pygmy goats calmed me." A blush line grew down his cheeks. "When I got home and realized it, Silas went to turn it off. He got here just in time to get the animals out." Benjamin's eyes were pleading now. "Can you ever forgive this wretched sinner?"

She nodded, stunned at the revelation. Barn fires were common, and the Amish didn't press charges, but simply built another one. Benjamin could have kept this a secret, and no one would ever know. This made Gracie respect him all the more. "Benjamin, your confession touches me. *Jah*, I forgive."

"Silas wanted to tell you, but I told him I needed to own up to my transgressions."

Gracie wanted to hug him but refrained herself. "You're being too hard on yourself. We confess, are forgiven, and move forward."

He nodded, relief washing over his face.

Leander was running from Gracie towards Leah. She

ran through the fields of flowers, but they looked back and laughed. The more she yelled for Leander to stop, to come to her, the further away he ran and was soon out of sight.

Cuckoo, cuckoo, cuckoo…

Gracie shot up, gasping for air, as the other clocks chimed. She oriented herself to see she was on the living room couch. Biting her lip to stop her chin from quivering, she swallowed hard. "What a silly dream," she told her dog who lay next to her. She rubbed his silky fur and tried to relax. "The man who gave you to me haunts me in my dreams!"

She glanced at the cuckoo clock with carved squirrels and acorns to see it was five o'clock. How long did she sleep? And why was she so tired? Why so sad? Gracie thought back to what a whirlwind the past few weeks had been since Leander's accident, and never did she crack open her Bible or bow her head in prayer. She prayed that Leander would live but strove to be still and confident that God was in control.

She got her Bible out of her unpacked suitcase as she rubbed her lower back. It was sore ever since Leander's accident. Feeling stressed, she bent over a few times to flex her taut muscles.

Flipping through her Bible, she landed on Psalms. One of her *Mamm*'s favorites was Psalm 47. She read:

*God is our refuge and strength, a very present help in trouble.*

*Therefore will not we fear, though the earth be removed, and though the mountains be carried into the midst of the sea;*

Like her *Mamm* would say, when the rug's pulled out from under you, don't fear, Gracie read the Psalm as a trickle of peace dripped in her heart.

*God is in the midst of her; she shall not be moved: God shall help her, and that right early.*

Lord, I want to be steady. Unshakable like *Mamm* and Granny Weaver. I'm just the opposite, like an earthquake in my heart.

And then she read, "Be still, and know that I am God" it seemed to jump off the page. It was a posture of submission and trust in God, her *Daed* always said. He modeled it well, too. His role as deacon caused him to struggle, but he would find a quiet place and calm down and return home determined to fulfill his duties. *Mamm* always mentioned that this is what drew her to him. She felt secure with a steadfast man who relied on God for stability. And his humility was unmatched. He didn't pretend to know all the answers, but simply trusted. He sought counsel, but in the end he was one man who truly trusted God.

"I want to be like *Daed*, Lord. Help me find a quiet

place…so I can quiet my soul. Give me a steady heart. One not cringing in fear about my future, but one with hope. Like you say, 'Surely goodness and mercy shall follow me all the days of my life'. You're the Good Shepherd and I trust you."

She shut her eyes tight when she thought of a shepherd. "And help me get over Leander!"

∞∞∞

When Gracie arrived at Maryann's house, the screen door flew open and her girlfriends ran to hug her. "We've missed you!" They said in unison and then laughed. They linked arms and entered the house. She jumped when several women shouted, "Welcome home!"

So moved, Gracie's eyes pulled tears. Each woman embraced her, but she gave Teresa an extra squeeze. She spied around to see Rachel, but she was absent. Why did this bother her? So many *gut* friends, but Rachel's absence poked at her.

Maryann took control of the party. "I've made a few pies, along with Teresa, and we're going to make ice cream with my new ice cream maker from Lehmans!"

Betty rubbed her middle. "I can eat for two."

"Are you having twins?" Gracie asked.

"*Nee,* I don't think so. I meant me and the *boppli. Ach,* Paul's so excited he's carving a cradle and will put the *boppli*'s name on it."

Chatter ensued and Gracie soon fell into comfortable conversation with many of these women she went to grade school with. Starved of close bosom friends, she told of her adventures in Smicksburg. Women's color choices for clothes made some bite their tongues, only to say that they hoped they'd be able to wear green someday. "Grass is green", Jenny said, "And God made it."

Many asked how Luke was, and she had to ask that they keep him in their prayers. She explained Leander's accident and when she did, many glanced at each other with suspicion.

"His *bruder* died, and Luke's close to the family. Leander's his best friend, and having no kin around, they're like *bruder*."

Teresa squirmed a bit. "Gracie, are you hot? Not feeling well?"

"What do you mean?"

"You're blushing to beat the band," Maria blurted. "Sounds like this Leander is your *gut* friend, too."

Gracie pretended to not understand their meaning. "He's like family to Luke, so I saw him a lot." She inhaled. "To be honest, I've been exhausted all day. I slept for near seven hours this afternoon."

"Stress build-up," Teresa said. "We lost *Mamm* and soon you were helping Abigail. And then a horrific accident. Do you know how it happened?"

"*Jah*. A drunk truck driver. He survived and many of the Amish went to tell him he's forgiven."

All heads nodded, knowing it was the Amish way to not press charges, but she knew they were thinking of Tim Yoder's family being killed by a drunk driver. "It's a real shame they drink so much alcohol. You'd think driving would make you tired and you'd drink lots of coffee."

Silence hung like a cloud, but Maryann lifted it when she asked who wanted to crank the ice cream maker. Betty put a hand up, but everyone was pampering her since she struggled to get around. Was she carrying twins, Gracie wondered.

"So, what's new in Cherry Creek?" Gracie asked.

"We made thousands of dollars at the annual auction. We made enough to pay for our insurance for the *kinner* for a year."

"Gracie," Jenny said, pressing her chest, "The colors in some quilts were…"

"Beyond beautiful," Maryann finished. "We here made a quilt that fetched eight-hundred dollars."

The pride the women showed warmed Gracie's heart. "I wish I could have been here to help."

"We'll be making another one," Maria said. "The item that fetched the highest price was a woodstove made by Benjamin and Silas Miller."

Baffled, Gracie blurted out, "But they don't know how to make a woodstove."

"John Hershberger taught them. They are huge. You can fit five logs in at a time and it heats the complete house."

"I've seen them," Gracie said, "But, you say they... donated a stove? They could have fetched at least three thousand for it."

Teresa pat Gracie's back. "Benjamin's a changed man. So is Silas."

Gracie didn't want to reveal seeing Benjamin, since his confession was private, but she was indeed shocked. "Silas was okay with donating?"

"Now, he's the changed man," Jenny said dreamily. "I always thought him handsome, but his character is so kind now that, well, at least I'm not afraid of him saying something rude."

"He better tone it down about his newfound faith, though," Maria said. "He's handing out religious tracks and asking everyone if they're born again."

"It's just his wording," Teresa defended. "He was an

atheist, so we should be glad he's come into the faith."

All heads nodded in agreement, except Jenny. "Well, word has it he went to an English church."

"What?" Maryann near screamed. "Are you sure?"

"*Nee,* not sure, but heard it through the grapevine."

"Then it's just a rumor, nothing more. Now, let's dish up some pies and you ladies can dig in. We have so much to catch up on."

Gracie rose to get a plate and decided on blackberry. How many times had she picked berries in the giant patch in the backyard? *Ach,* such *gut* times. So glad to be home, yet her heart was torn. Maybe Teresa was right. Over the past months, she'd experienced excessive stress. Having the house all to herself, she was grateful to have a quiet place to recover.

The next day, Shep's deep growl woke her up. She instantly knew by the slant of the sunrays that she'd slept in. *Am I sick?* She threw on her robe, put a bandana over her hair, and descended the steps to see what was upsetting Shep. When she saw Silas, she ran into the utility room, twirled her hair and stuffed it under the bandana. She was prepared to greet the man who could be her husband.

When she placed her hand on the doorknob, Shep crouched down and barked something fierce. "What's wrong with you?" She grabbed a leash that was hanging on the wooden peg board and fastened it. "Sit down."

Silas opened the door and it took all of Gracie's might to hold back her dog. "I'm sorry. He's never acted this way."

Silas knelt down in front of Shep and let him smell his hand. "He doesn't know me yet. He thinks I'm a threat. Calm down, now. I won't hurt you."

Soon Shep was his usual self, but that Silas didn't yell or get irritated with the dog astonished her. "I'm sorry, Silas. He's real gentle."

Silas smiled. "Getting over being a hothead takes time," he winked. "I'll teach him. I've got practice." He rolled his eyes. "Sorry, I forgot something. I need to go to the buggy."

When he was gone, Gracie tried to get over the embarrassment of being in her pajamas. She eyed the clock, and it was nine-thirty. Gracie covered her mouth in shock. What impression will my laziness make on Silas?

Silas soon appeared with a bouquet of roses. "For you. Roses for a girl as sweet...as roses." He hit his head. "That was corny." He opened his arms and hugged her tight. "I've missed you. I'm so relieved you're back home."

"Relieved?" she whispered.

"I'm afraid of that other guy. Are you going to write to him?"

The insecurity in his voice made Gracie realize how much he cared. She fetched a vase for the flowers. "Leander is badly hurt. I'm not sure he's up for reading letters."

Silas took a seat at the table. Coffee was brewing and sticky buns were taken out of the icebox. "Let's have breakfast. I can't believe I slept so long. I've been plumb exhausted."

"Do you need to see a doctor?"

"Everyone says I've been through too much stress and that will cause fatigue."

"It wouldn't hurt for you to see a doc. I've never known you to be exhausted. I see the dark lines under your eyes."

Gracie blushed. "I've noticed them, too. Getting old."

"Now, did I say you look old Gracie Hershberger? Never. You're as fresh as..."

"Spring rain?" Gracie said with a laugh.

"That you are. Like spring rain."

They held each other's gaze for a spell. "I'm glad to be

back home," she managed to say.

He took her hand. "I never realized how much you mean to me until you left. It gave me time to face reality.... to face myself and change."

"I heard you made a woodstove and donated it to the auction. That's some donation."

Silas beamed and straightened. "*Daed* and I did it. We work together when we're not out roofing or tending to the cows. You should come over and see the changes to the house."

"I heard," Gracie let slip. "*Ach,* I'm sorry. Your *daed* stopped over yesterday to talk."

"About what?"

Confessions were personal, but it bothered her that Benjamin pushed his son to marry her. "Well, your *daed* confessed a few things. Said he pushed you to marry me for the farm—"

"That's not true, Gracie. I mean, he pushed me, but I didn't need it. Do you still think I want you for this house and farm?"

She studied him and saw sincerity. "*Nee,* not anymore. Anyhow, I want to see Teresa and William have it."

"That's *gut* of you. But where will you live?"

"*Ach,* it won't happen for a while. And I'm not too lonely here with Shep." She rose to pour coffee.

"And I'm trying to believe Psalm 23. That God is my shepherd and will lead me."

He thanked her for the coffee and took a sip. "Gracie, that New Testament you gave me made me so thirsty for the Bible, I got a new one. It's a study Bible in a translation I can understand."

"Really? Did the bishop approve?"

He shrugged his shoulders. "Never asked."

"It's probably nothing, but I'd show him. I learned from the English that some translations aren't too *gut*."

"Well, I like this one, but if it makes you happy, I'll show the bishop. Now, how about you get yourself ready while I take the tape off your buggy?"

"Tape off my buggy?"

"I'm done painting it. Marked off areas so I wouldn't get paint on the seat."

"*Danki*, Silas. I thought Bruce did it." She wanted to run around the table and hug him, but her feet felt like lead. *What is wrong with me?*

# Chapter 17

G racie accepted Silas' offer to take a buggy ride to catch up and then visit his house. Seeing her old stomping ground made her appreciate its beauty. No curvy roads around rolling hills, but the Allegheny mountains towering up from flat land. She wondered if this was the reason most Amish farmed in New York. Flat land was rare in Smicksburg. The massive barns impressed her as if seeing them for the first time. The houses, two or three connecting as families grew, and some added on to be near kin or help on the farm. How she loved Cherry Creek. Smicksburg had its charm, especially all the shops and conversing with the English, but this was home. 'Grow where you're planted' she could almost hear her *Mamm* say.

When they arrived at Silas' house, Gracie's eyes bugged. "What happened?"

"What happened? Gracie Hershberger, don't you

like it?"

"I love it. It looks new."

He helped her out of the buggy and held her hand as they neared the house. In no time, Benjamin and his wife, Tillie, were on the massive front porch.

"Welcome home, Gracie," Tillie gushed. "What's your opinion of our new place?"

She tried to take in the new white siding and black metal roof, new windows...everything. "It looks like a new house."

"Well, the bones are still in there," Benjamin said with a laugh. "Despite the house being over a century old, it remains solid, with only a few floorboards needing replacement."

Gracie glanced at the grove of trees that used to be near the house. "Did you have a storm? I remember playing in the trees as a kid."

Silas took her hand and squeezed them tight. "We'll build a house there, next to my parents." He winked. "See, I didn't want you for your farm."

Tillie enveloped them both. "God answers prayer. My husband is a new man, as is my son. We have a Christian home, reading the Bible every night together. When you two wed, we'll have many winter days to keep each other company."

Not knowing what to say, and her mouth too dry to

utter anything, she only nodded.

"Come inside and see my new kitchen," Tillie said.

Upon entering, the shiny oak floors made Gracie gawk. "Who did this?"

"Andy Troyer, the best carpenter in the area. All the floors are new. They even smell new, don't you think?"

"I do." Gracie pointed at the room, "You used to have a wall in here. Now it's just one big room?"

"More spacious. And the windows are bigger, too."

Gracie was at a loss for words upon discovering white sheers in the back. This was breaking the Amish code. Her expression must have given her away since Tillie explained that more sunlight from the wide windows made them use less lamp oil. Gracie dropped the matter and walked to the far side of the house as Tillie near danced around her large kitchen, now remodeled with cherry cabinets and a granite countertop.

"It's real granite, not the fake kind," Benjamin boasted. "Got a *gut* deal from an Englisher friend in Salamanca."

Gracie staggered to the kitchen table. "You have English friends?"

"*Jah*, I do. I'm real fond of some of the Native Americans I do business with."

Silas sat next to Gracie. "Not casino friends."

Benjamin laughed. "Gracie, you look as pale as a snowman. What do you take me for? I'm a repentant man. No liquor, no gambling, and a happy wife to boot." He put an arm around Tillie and their heads touched.

"Are you okay, Gracie?" Silas asked.

"I keep getting dizzy spells and fatigue comes on without warning."

"We're going to see the herbalist doc, unless you want to see Doctor Mast, the Mennonite doctor."

"I think she needs to have some blood tests. Might be anemic," Tillie said.

Gracie raised a hand in protest. "It's stress."

"When I was a sinner, I got so tired from anxiety it near did me in. But the Lord lifted me up." Benjamin said with feeling.

"I don't think Gracie is a sinner for having stress," Silas defended. "She's been through a lot in the past few months." He squeezed her hand. "It wouldn't hurt to get some bloodwork done, though."

She felt lightheaded and lay her head on the table. "That would be *gut*."

When Gracie entered Dr. Mast's office, the beautifully framed cross-stitch flowers amazed her. "His wife makes them. They're Mennonite and are allowed to do so much we can't," Silas said under his breath as they took seats.

"We're allowed to do needlework, it's just that many women don't. I learned how to spin yarn in Smicksburg." She eyed the flowers again. "*Mamm* loved roses. Can I make something like that?"

"Maybe Flora Mast can teach you."

"*Jah*, maybe she can." Gracie was comforted by Silas' care. She felt loved. But, how could someone change so fast?

Silas rose when a middle-aged woman came into the empty waiting room. "Hi Flora. This is my girl, and she's been having fatigue and dizzy spells. Can the doc do bloodwork to rule out anemia?"

Flora offered Gracie her hand. "Nice to meet you. And your name is?"

"Gracie. Gracie Hershberger."

"Well, Gracie, my husband will be back soon. Someone called him out to deliver her baby. The problem is, this woman is so nervous, she's done this seven days in a row. Her husband looks like a scared rabbit." Flora laughed gently. "But it's their first child."

"Gracie loves all your cross-stitch flowers. Can you

teach her?"

"Well, of course I can. We can start with something simple. Counted cross-stitch can be tricky and some give up."

"Gracie loves crafts. She can spin yarn."

Flora squealed. "For real?"

Gracie nodded. "Unfortunately, I don't have a spinning wheel here. I learned in Pennsylvania."

"I've always wanted to crochet a sweater or vest to wear. Can you make a cable stitch?"

"*Jah*," Gracie said. "We can buy yarn in Randolph. Some spun yarn is uneven, at least mine is, and I wouldn't want you to get discouraged."

"We'll both be newbies in a new craft. Can't wait." She tilted her head. "I think my husband's here. Heard the car door shut. Follow me into one of the patient rooms."

∞ ∞ ∞

When Silas took Gracie home, he insisted she rest. He kissed her on the forehead and said he'd tell Rachel help was needed. Gracie protested, so he said he'd let her tell her *schwestern*. When he closed the door, she flung herself on the couch. *Ach*, rest? If I sleep more,

I'll sleep all the time.

She eyed the stamped cross-stitch kittens. It was kind of Silas to take her to Randolph to buy this new craft. The nine squares each had a different kitten, some holding teacups, some swinging, some running in a field. She squelched down the thought of making this for her own *boppli*. Most likely she'd make the quilt squares into a blanket for Betty or Rachel's *boppli*.

As much as she tried, her heart continued to sink. She'd know her test results in a few days, but a lack of Vitamin D was clear to the doctor. When he asked if she was depressed, she was ashamed to tell the truth. She had faith in God. When he said he noticed it, she felt shame. His kind words about grief, losing her *Mamm* and being alone in the house was only half of her sorrow. How could she tell him she missed Leander and felt betrayed? Silas paraded her around as his girlfriend a bit too much.

Gracie made some chamomile tea and sat in her rocker. Once situated, she started a gratitude list. The doc said it helped combat depression. So, she picked up her notebook and wrote:

*Silas and Benjamin have changed for the better. A miracle of sorts.*

*Silas taking me to the craft store.*

*Silas taking me to the doctor.*

She stopped. Everything revolved around Silas after she saw him. She thought of her friends surprising her with a welcome home party and she continued to write about each friend by name. The more she wrote an abundance of blessings were all around her. She just needed to choose to see them.

Her heart lifted. She'd move forward and not look back. It wasn't worth her health to fret over Leander. She wrote one more thing in her notebook. *Glad to be home.*

∞ ∞ ∞

*Dear Gracie,*

*I hope you're not missing me too much. Abigail and Alice say hi.*

*I wanted to give you an update on Leander. Thank God he's going to make it. Only the elders knew all the injuries and outcomes since they approve payments. We have no lack since it got into the Budget and more than enough came in from a card shower. He's not as sedated and he talks just fine now. He said the drugs made him feel crazy. Steroids made him nervous. He asked where you were and I said you went back home. Maybe it's my imagination, but he looked mighty down.*

*Anyhow, Leander might need a liver transplant. It's not official yet. I don't understand all the stuff about enzymes and whatnot, but if he doesn't improve, he'll need a transplant. I'm glad his heart is fine, since we Amish don't get heart transplants after baptism. (Never understood that one.) Leander and I are the same blood type and I told him I'd donate a part of mine. So did half of the Gmay, so maybe I won't be a match. He may not even need it. Maybe I shouldn't tell you but he needs prayer. Tell the Amish up there to pray for my best buddy.*

*Now, as your twin I know that you're crying. Please, don't. I want to tell you something awesome about Leander. He's had lots of stitches and some skin grafts. They asked him if he wanted his port wine stain to be covered at no charge, and he said no. Jeb Weaver said the cost was so minimal that if he wanted to have it, he'd be behind him. But Leander said God made him with the stain and it needs to stay.*

*I know you're upset about Leah being with the family so much. Abigail asked her and she only said she was close to the family and sobbed. Abigail said she won't be asking again.*

*Are you still waiting until wedding season to accept Silas? I hope you wait. Marriage is forever and I want you to marry the one God intended. Maybe it's Silas, maybe it's not.*

*Please write back and let me know how you are.*

*Miss you,*

*Luke*

Gracie held the letter to her heart. Luke be a liver donor? What was he thinking? She knew he'd only give half of his, the liver growing back to normal size in a few months, but what if something went wrong?

She clenched her fist. This was the worst news. Why did Luke tell her? Of course, he thought she was fine and dandy after being home. Maybe Rachel or Teresa wrote and told him she looked good. But she didn't feel good.

# Chapter 18

The next day, she received another letter from Smicksburg:

Dear Aunt Gracie,

*I miss you! The house is so empty without you.*

*I hear Leander might be coming home in a couple weeks. He'll need help. Maybe you can come and help. His parents look so tired. Mamm took over a meal and I went with her. Ruth asked about you. She said you were as sweet as pie and hoped to see you soon. I think that was her way of hinting that she wanted you to help her.*

*I think the sheep miss Leander. Boaz is taking care of them, but he looks like an old man. Can men get gray hair because they're sad? I saw him crying out in the field. He misses his son. I'm so glad both of his sons weren't taken.*

*Write back and let me know if you need me to come up and stay with you again. I just love you and hope I grow up just like you.*

*Alice*

∞ ∞ ∞

Even though Gracie was home for a week, she continued to have dizzy spells and fatigue. The doc gave her Vitamin D since her bloodwork showed it was low. Everything else was normal. Stress, anxiety and depression were what he suspected. She still cringed at the thought. She was a strong woman. How could she be depressed?

She read Psalms like her *Mamm* did. She said they were songs that helped her express her emotions. The doctor recommended sunlight for natural Vitamin D production in the body. So on this June day, she put on her sneakers and would walk to Teresa's house.

It was a rare sunny day, not a cloud in the sky, and she breathed in the scent of lavender. She learned about essential oils, specifically lavender as a calming tonic. Breathing deeply was also suggested by the doc. He said while under stress we can forget to breathe. As she walked, she didn't know if it was her imagination, but her mood seemed to improve. Her parents would instruct her, as a child, to go for a walk and clear her mind of cobwebs. Gracie smiled at the memory. She'd blush, thinking they could read her mind and could see some of her bad thoughts that needed cleaned out.

"*Ach, Mamm* and *Daed*, I hope you see me. Angels can see us, so why can't you?"

She saw a black car approaching and she gasped. Silas? What was he doing with the Mennonites? They stopped by the roadside and Silas jumped out. "Can we give you a lift?"

Gracie pulled him aside to have a private word. "Silas, why so cozy with the Mennonites? You know they try to get the Amish to jump the fence."

"And some Mennonites turn Amish," he retorted. "Do you need a ride?"

"I'm walking to Teresa's," she said, pointing in the opposite direction. "And I enjoy walking."

An uneasiness hung between them. He rushed to the car and returned. "I asked them to wait a minute. Gracie, you look upset."

"I'm not upset, I'm shocked. We're to stick to our own kind. They may pull you away from the Amish."

His face grew solemn. "They have the best Bible studies and help people more than the Amish."

She covered her mouth. "Silas. The Amish show our love for God by living in a community. Are you out preaching? I heard you were."

He slipped a tract out of his pocket. "We give these out. I don't preach. I just hand these to people to read.

Is there any harm in that?"

She shifted. "I guess not."

He took her by the shoulders. "I'm baptized Amish. I am Amish. Trust me."

His eyes were soft and sincere. No trace of arrogance remained. She nodded. "I do trust you, Silas. Have a *gut* day."

"Can I see you tonight? I have a surprise."

She smiled. "*Jah*. How about we make ice cream?"

"Yummy."

She watched the car pull away and marveled. It seemed like Silas found what he was looking for. They weren't forbidden to have Mennonite friends. She didn't know any except the doctor and his wife. And Flora was visiting tomorrow. The Amish in Smicksburg had many English friends, and she wasn't tempted once to want fancy things. Silas wouldn't either.

∞∞∞

When she reached Teresa's house, she found her sister in a fluster. "I got a letter from Luke. He's talking about being a liver donor. *Ach,* we need to talk him out of it."

Gracie tried to soothe her. "He wrote to me, too. He said many men and women in their *Gmay* were getting tested. I doubt he'll be a match."

"Women? Aren't they afraid their *kinner* will be without a *Mamm*? Isn't Luke afraid that he'll leave Abigail a widow?"

Gracie had never seen her sister in such a flurry and had to admit she was glad to see it. Teresa was so calm, and it was nice to see her sister not so stoic. "Luke will be fine. It's done all the time."

"I know all about it, but it's not like Leander is kin. Doesn't he have kin who could donate?"

William walked into the kitchen and wrapped his arms around his wife. "It's going to be okay. Your little *bruder* is an adult and will make the right decision."

She leaned into him. "I know. It's just that I—"

"This of yourself as their *Mamm* now?"

She turned to hug him. "I miss *Mamm* and *Daed*'s advice."

William held her a spell and then they sat around the table to have lemonade.

"Have you heard anything from the realtor?" William asked.

Gracie arched a brow. "I forgot all about selling the farm."

His eyes met his wife's. "Well, Teresa's real fond of

the place. We built this house together and she found it hard to admit she wanted to move. But, if you decide to sell, I think we'd be interested."

Gracie nearly choked with emotion. Their love was all she desired. "You'd do that for Teresa? You just put a new metal roof on your place. For ten years, you have been fertilizing your fields.

He took Teresa's hand. "Teresa's never felt at home here."

"*Jah*, I don't know why. But when I go to *Mamm* and *Daed*'s I feel like I'm supposed to be there."

Gracie shared what she learned from Doctor Mast about grief. "Doc Mast said I'm dealing with grief. Something about stress buildup too. My fatigue and dizzy spells could all be depression and anxiety. Stress can disrupt the body, it not being able to take in Vitamin D. My bloodwork showed mine is very low."

"Is that why you're pale?" Teresa asked.

"I don't know. But I need sunshine. Can you believe sunshine provides Vitamin D? I'm also eating more fish. I'm learning to like tuna fish sandwiches."

Teresa put her hand up. "Are you saying grief might be affecting me?"

William nodded. "I know it is. You were a close-knit family. It's okay to cry about your *mamm*. You're always trying to be strong for other people except yourself."

She hugged his neck. "I need to be strong."

"*Nee,* Teresa," Gracie said. "You've got to let your sorrow out. It's not healthy."

"Honey, will you see Doc Mast?"

"*Jah,* William. I will. Gracie thank you ever so much."

The two sisters embraced.

∞∞∞

Gracie poured two cups of lemonade into glass tumblers and placed it on the tray near the cookies. Why she wanted to show Amish hospitality to Flora, a Mennonite, pricked her. What was she trying to prove? She placed the tray on the small cedar wood table that was between two chairs. "Hope you like lemon tarts."

"Oh, I like anything lemon," Flora said. "It's so refreshing. This June is hot, don't you think?"

"It's exhausting. I can't handle 80-degree weather."

"We're used to much cooler weather." Flora bit into a tart. "Oh, my. My taste buds are dancing."

Gracie cocked her head. "Dance? Do Mennonites dance?"

"Some do, but we're fairly conservative here. There's

as many types of Mennonites as there are ice cream." Flora beamed. "How about the Amish?"

"There's eight levels of strictness," Gracie informed. "We're Troyer Amish in New York, much stricter than the Andy Weaver Amish where my *bruder* lives."

"What do the names mean?"

"*Ach,* the man who started the different Amish group call themselves by their new founder's name."

Flora grinned. "The Amish broke from the Mennonites."

"*Jah*, I know. When I visited Smicksburg the Amish were much…I can't describe it."

"Freer?"

"*Jah*. Freer to wear pleasant colors. I saw someone wear lavender."

"What I mean by freedom is freedom to read the Bible. Believe in what it says."

Gracie's eyes bugged. "Many Amish, including myself, have a Bible. I read it every day. Most families have Bible reading at night."

Flora opened her mouth and then put a finger to her lips. "We have different beliefs. Let's just leave it at that. I came to teach you to cross stitch and for me to learn how to crochet." She reached into the plaid tote near her chair. "Isn't this the prettiest yarn? It's part alpaca."

Gracie ran her fingers through the fibers. "It's thick. This is super chunky yarn. Did you get a crochet hook that's the right size?"

Flora mushed her lips together and then held up a tiny hook. "Will this do?"

Gracie laughed. "That's for lace. The size hook you need is written on the yarn." Gracie pointed to the instructions on the yarn label. "I always use the recommended size, but some use bigger if they want a looser stitch."

Flora slumped. "I was excited to start today."

"No problem. I have every hook size. My twin is such a *gut* carver, and he made me some hooks. Let me get them." Since Gracie kept all her hooks in a little basket nearby, she was back in a flash. "Look at this one."

Flora admired the hook. "It has a mushroom carved on the end. How adorable."

"*Jah*. Luke is gifted with his hands."

Flora seemed deep in thought. "My mom was Amish, and she used a horse and buggy. My dad always wonders if the Mennonites made a mistake allowing cars. I don't know. The world seems so fast-paced. I see it in my husband's business. 'Patients need patience' he says sometimes when frustrated."

Gracie didn't want to pry, but wondered if her mom was shunned and what affect it had on her extended family. She tried to stay casual. "Want to return to horse and buggy?"

Flora grinned. "Sometimes. There are Horse and Buggy Mennonite in parts of Pennsylvania and Ohio. But the grass is greener on the other side. I appreciate my car on winter days. How do you Amish keep warm?"

"You've seen our buggy robes, *jah*?"

"Yes, but your buggies aren't enclosed like the Lancaster Amish."

Gracie knew Flora was poking fun. "We have curtains we roll down. I think it's snug."

Flora eyed the crochet hooks. "Which one should I use. I didn't come to challenge Amish ways."

"You don't challenge me. I love Amish ways. Now, look at the letter on the label."

"It's a K."

"Then find a K hook."

It only took ten minutes to teach Flora how to lace the yarn through her left fingers and make a chain stitch. Gracie recommended that she practice over and over until her stitches were even. Flora taught Gracie how to cross-stitch her stamped kitten quilt squares, which Gracie did with ease. They chattered on about many topics, and Gracie could see why Silas felt so comfortable around the Mennonites. It was only when Flora invited her to a woman's Bible study that Gracie felt awkward. Amish were forbidden to go to Bible studies outside the Amish church.

# Chapter 19

Gracie was in her backyard among her pygmy goats. The little things gave her a pint of milk a day and she tried her hand at making goat milk soap. She took her three-legged stool and started her task, talking to each goat, soothing them so they'd give more milk. Her mind wandered to Leander and his shepherd heart. He loved his sheep and he inspired her to talk to her goats.

Leander. Would she ever stop thinking of him? A mockingbird perched on a nearby tree, raising its wings, hopping, and singing a pleasant melody. *My heart will sing again, just like you.*

Who was acting real, Silas or Leander? She believed Leander was truly himself, especially after objecting to a skin graft to cover his birthmark. It was admirable and rare for someone to be comfortable with themselves. Truth be told, she'd met no one like Leander. Did he pop into her life to teach her a lesson? Many lessons?

She gasped for breath, not realizing she'd stopped breathing. Whenever she thought of Leander, she tried to squelch any feelings. He was far away, while Silas was near. Most likely he was courting Leah again and gave no thought about her.

A horse neighed and she noticed someone came for a visit. She sunk when she saw her sister, Rachel, hitch her horse to the post. She seemed to march towards Gracie.

"Gracie, we need to talk."

Blunt and to the point as ever. She knew some kind of rebuke or correction was coming. "I need to finish milking my goats."

"I'll only stay a few minutes. Have lots of wash to do." She eyed Gracie's clothesline. "Why isn't your wash up today. It's Monday."

"It's only me living here, so I wash every other Monday."

"You have over seven dresses?"

Should she dare say she made a green one? Yes, she needed to stand up to this sister. "I've made more. One is green."

Rachel nearly fell over. "You're not allowed to wear green here."

"I made it in Smicksburg and wear it around the house, not in public. But, when I visit Luke, I'll take it."

She held Rachel's glare.

"Well, it's bad enough that your beau is in trouble, and now you're wearing green? What is becoming of Old Order Amish ways?"

Gracie frowned. "Why would Silas be in trouble?"

"It happened yesterday after church. He got a talking to about being a sidewalk preacher."

Gracie groaned. "He only hands out religious tracts. And they don't contradict the *Dordrecht Confession of Faith.*"

"You've read them?"

"*Jah*, I did. Silas is teaching is what our original founders taught. Read the *Confession of Faith* and you'll see."

"B-But, we're not supposed to be out winning souls like the Mennonites. Our entire community shows the teachings of Christ. Love one another so people will see we're Christians by our actions."

"*Jah*, I agree. Why not do both? When I was in Smicksburg, I made some English friends who were Baptist. And they believe like we do. Like *Mamm* and *Daed* brought us up. *Mamm* read her Bible every day, so what's wrong with sharing it with others."

"It shows pride," Rachel croaked out. "You know that. *Mamm* kept her religious views to herself."

Gracie rose. "What do you want, Rachel? Did you

come to quarrel?"

Rachel pressed a hand against her forehead. "Am I talking to my little *schwester*? You aren't yourself."

Gracie ignored her and asked again about Silas.

"Well, he seems to be daft about his preaching ways. Said he saw nothing wrong with it and is refusing to stop preaching."

"He's not preaching. He's just sharing literature. Many Amish communities do that. And look at our Amish newspapers like *Family Life.* So many share stories about how their lives were changed by their spiritual growth." Gracie kept digging in her heels. "And we Amish all read the *Foxe's Book of Martyrs* daily so we don't forget how our forefathers suffered for their faith, and we can expect the same."

Rachel spun around and headed to her buggy. She looked back and shouted, "Gracie, someone has bewitched you."

Bewitched? Gracie laughed at Rachel's dramatic ways, but she had changed. Before, she never stood up for her beliefs. Perhaps Smicksburg gave her a fresh view of Amish life.

Shortly after Rachel's departure, another buggy arrived in the driveway. Silas appeared and hooked the horse to the hitching post. Hands in his pockets and shoulders slumped, he gingerly made his way to her.

"I think some of my goats are pregnant, "Gracie said. "I've never had to deal with birthing."

He sat on a barn stool. "I'm sure there's many that can help you."

Gracie had never heard Silas' tone so forlorn.

"I need your advice. The bishop came down hard on me. I'd say, on the Gospel of Jesus. Why should I keep quiet when I know that being born again has changed me? God's spirit lives in me, shaping me."

Gracie inhaled and prayed for wisdom. "Maybe it's the wording. I never heard anyone say they're born again except the ones who go door to door. They're insulting to most Amish. They think we have no access to Bibles or maybe aren't educated. I remember my *Oma* being quite taken back by some of them."

Silas picked up a piece of straw and fiddled with it. "I know some are very arrogant who've come to our house, but the Mennonites aren't. And Jesus said you cannot see the kingdom of heaven if you're not born again."

Gracie wanted to mention his neglected upbringing, but she tried to be tactful. "I've only known that

Jesus loves me since a wee one. We had Bible reading near every night, and my *daed* would read from the *Dordecht Confession of Faith*. It says that our names are written in heaven upon repentance and renewal by the Holy Spirit." She paused, remembering something. "That was written by Mennonites. We broke away from them because we thought they were getting too worldly with cars and such, but we share the same beliefs."

Silas's eyes met hers, and Gracie saw his eyes flame. "How come nobody told me that? Why don't the Amish teach this?"

"Silas, they don't even teach the Bible in our one-room schools. It's the parents sacred duty to teach their *kinner*."

"And it's the church preachers, too. I grasp their preaching now, but their sayings are overly fearful. Too much about hell and being hammered to be perfect."

Befuddled, Gracie kept quiet a spell. She let her fingers run down the white goat's fur, and it leaned into her. "Silas, I know you've always feared your *daed*. Do you see your heavenly father in the same way?"

"That's what the Mennonites say. Amish follow the law but lack faith."

"Silas, did you even hear my question? I don't care

what the Mennonites think. Did you grow up fearing God in an unhealthy way?"

"Well, it's been pounded into us we'll go to hell if we leave the Amish."

Gracie gasped. "I don't hear that. Anyhow, there's so many kinds of Amish, which one is right?"

He nodded. "*Gut* point. The Amish up here are too strict. I hear there's a branch in Holmes County that's called New Order. Do I belong there?"

An avalanche of emotion rocked Gracie. "What? Move to Ohio? You're baptized here."

Silas raked his fingers through his hair. "Gracie, I can't deny how much my faith has changed me."

"I see that. But the Good Book says faith without works is dead, *jah*? We Amish show our faith through our works. Our taking in the orphans, as so many are foster parents. We live in community, in unity, and I dare say that would be impossible if it wasn't for our faith. We believe in forgiveness, submission, charity. Silas, maybe the family you grew up in wasn't a *gut* example." She cupped her mouth. "Silas, I'm sorry."

He reached for her hand. "It's okay. I wasn't raised like most Amish. I've got a chip on my shoulder about that." He squeezed her hand as if for dear life. "Will you try to understand where I'm coming from. Will you go to a Mennonite church down the road?"

She didn't want him to be shunned. She needed to help him see both ways and she was sure once he got over his painful upbringing, he'd see God as a loving heavenly father. "*Jah*, Silas. Just once."

He kissed her hands and tears fell. "I know you're taking a risk. No one's loved me like you, Gracie."

She hugged him. "Don't go and get yourself shunned."

∞∞∞

Gracie felt ashamed that she and Silas had to sneak around the back of the church, after the black car drove into the parking lot. Reflecting on the verse, 'Be as gentle as a dove but as wise as a serpent,' had been her focus. In order to prevent him from being deceived, she had to support Silas. In addition to needing to be kind, she had to be wise.

Upon entering the red brick church, a heavenly song pierced the air. "What is that?"

"A cello," Doc Mast informed.

"The man who plays the violin is superb," Flora added.

*This music is heavenly*, Gracie thought.

When they took their seat among the shiny oak

213

pews, Gracie looked around. Whole families were sitting together. No separation of male and female. Could boyfriend and girlfriend sit together?

The church service started with singing. Some songs Gracie heard in Smicksburg at Suzy's knitting store. *Amazing Grace* and *There's Power in the Blood.* When they sang other songs, she had the hymnal to guide her and was uplifted. After twenty minutes of worship, the pastor took his pulpit. He asked any newcomers to raise their hand, which Gracie reluctantly did. However, she saw two Amish individuals among the others. Most likely on rumspringa, but she was baptized. The shock on one girl's face was accusing.

Shaken, she tried to pay attention to what the pastor said. He read Psalm 23, and Gracie cringed. David's psalm about the Good Shepherd. The pastor asked them to read it aloud together.

*The Lord is my shepherd; I shall not want.*

*He maketh me to lie down in green pastures: he leadeth me beside the still waters.*

*He restoreth my soul: he leadeth me in the paths of righteousness for his name's sake.*

*Yea, though I walk through the valley of the shadow of death, I will fear no evil: for thou art with me; thy rod and thy staff they comfort me.*

*Thou preparest a table before me in the presence of mine enemies: thou anointest my head with oil; my cup runneth over.*

*Surely goodness and mercy shall follow me all the days of my life: and I will dwell in the house of the Lord forever.*

Gracie held on to the pew, feeling weak. Leander's words came to mind. *I want to be your shepherd. I have experience…some sheep are hard to earn their trust.*

She near rebuked the image of him out of her mind. He had no right intruding on her thoughts. He was with Leah, and she had to live in the practical, here in Cherry Creek with Silas. But memories flooded her, the more she tried to keep them at bay. She attempted to listen to the preacher and was clear-headed enough to hear any heresy. After the half hour sermon, she found nothing she didn't agree with.

She noticed how Silas was beaming. She overheard him saying to Flora that he was starting to understand that God was personal and really his shepherd and he'd lead him in his church matters. What did that mean?

# Chapter 20

Early the next morning, Maryann flung open the side screen door and darted to the table, sitting next to Gracie. "Tell me it isn't true."

She yawned. "What's not true?"

"That you went to the Mennonite Church. Silas is not right for you. Why would he ask you to do that?"

Gracie gawked. "Last night. How did you know?"

"The Amish grapevine is ready to catch fire. How could you, Gracie? You vowed to be Amish."

She shifted. "I went to protect Silas." Thoughts of being single, alone her whole life, choked her. She sipped her coffee for comfort. "I help steady him. It's just a phase for him. He's Amish."

Maryann slid closer to her friend. "I know you and am so concerned. You'll marry Silas because he's familiar..."

"Shouldn't he be? Should I marry someone I hardly know?"

"Are you talking about Leander in Smicksburg?"

Gracie's cheeks burned. "Smicksburg is a fantasy. I wish I'd never gone. The Amish there are so free. Mix with Baptists, friends with many English. I'm here in Cherry Creek and it's my world."

"Do you still care for Leander?"

Gracie bit back tears. "*Jah*, I do. But I don't really know him."

"And you know Silas, but who do you trust? Who do you think has the best character?"

"What difference does it make? Leander said he'd write to me and hasn't. He forgot me already. Living down there was like a dream. No work, responsibilities. It was a vacation and I met friendly folk."

"Who's the lady you talked to for advice?"

"Granny Weaver," Gracie near whispered. "I miss her."

"Maybe Leander has reasons to doubt you. Silas visited you and you came right back home. Didn't stay to help Leander's parents."

Gracie clenched her fists. "Leah, with her constant sobbing and clinging to Ruth and Boaz crowded me out. Obviously, they're a couple."

They sat in silence. Shep lay his head on Gracie's feet, and she thought of the day Leander brought him to her. *Such happy times. Such hopeful times.*

"Isn't Luke his best friend?" Maryann asked.

"*Jah*, they're like *bruder*."

"Does Luke know how you feel?"

Gracie felt fatigue wash over her. Stress was taking its toll. "His wife, Abigail, asked why Leah was always at Leander's parent's house, and was met with resistance. Obviously, they have a secret courting going on."

Maryann bit into her sticky bun. "Word has it that Joe Byler's looking for a wife. His *kinner* need a *Mamm*. Too bad Esther was taken."

Gracie eyed her friend. "He's nearly forty. Maybe fifty. His *kinner* are older."

Maryann suppressed a laugh. "I'm sorry. I was just teasing...sort of."

"Sort of? *Ach*, Maryann, you know me. I'd never marry a man I didn't love."

Maryann arched a brow. "So, you love Silas?"

Why couldn't she say it out loud? She wasn't committing to a marriage proposal...yet.

∞∞∞

Later that day, Gideon Miller, the deacon, stopped over with his wife. Gracie knew what was coming.

They sat around the table, coffee mugs filled and cookies within reach.

"It's a nice July day, *jah*?" Barbara asked.

"*Jah*. Hard to believe it's July already."

"How's your garden coming along?"

"*Ach*, my kitchen garden is *gut*. Getting lots of tomatoes this year."

Gideon readjusted his straw hat. "Gracie, Emily Yoder told us she saw you in the Mennonite church. She's our neighbor and felt she needed to say something."

Gracie appreciated this kind deacon. He didn't mention the whole town knew. "*Jah*, I was there. I'm courting Silas and he asked me to go. We've been talking about his new birth, and I told him we believe the same."

"Well, we don't assume we're so-called saved. What if we say that and then turn our backs on Jesus?"

Gracie pressed her chest. "When you know him inside, you have that assurance of eternal life. Peter said to Jesus, 'You have the words of eternal life'. I think —"

"You preach to me?" Gideon boomed.

Startled, Gracie felt defensive. "My parents had daily Bible reading. We talked about it freely and we discussed it. I'm just discussing it with you."

Barbara put a hand on her husband's shoulder. "We're concerned about you Gracie. We don't want you being one of those Christians who come to our doors. They tell us to say a simple prayer and then go off and live like the devil."

Gracie knew who she referred to. The family claimed to be born again Christians, but their life didn't align.

Gideon opened his Bible to the Book of James. "We believe that faith without works is dead."

The presence of her parents seemed to blanket Gracie. She knew this scripture, but also knew that good works resulted from faith. How many times had her *Mamm* said she'd never be able to bear her crosses if it wasn't for her faith. "Faith empowers us to do good," she said. Gracie grabbed a black book from a shelf. "It's written in the *Dordrecht Confession of Faith, Article 7*. Concerning baptism we confess that all penitent believers, who, through faith, regeneration, and the renewing of the Holy Ghost, are made one with God, and are written in heaven—"

"Stop!" Gideon bellowed. "Gracie that's the Mennonite belief."

"But, we still study and abide by it. I grew up on it. You took my *daed*'s place as deacon. Did you know him?"

He sighed. "*Jah*, I did. He was free about his beliefs

and at first, he made me nervous. But he taught me much."

Barbara leaned forward as if telling a secret. "We loved your *daed*. Many of us believe as you do. We know Jesus and his love. But we don't evangelize. We live it out. Ever wonder why the English are drawn to the Amish? Some say we point to God by our works and faith. You see, you need both."

Gracie felt like this was splitting hairs, but she nodded, needing time to think.

Gideon forced a smile. "We'll be watching you over the next few weeks. A proving of sorts. A shepherd must look after his sheep." His eyes brimmed. "And no seeing Silas. He's been talked to and is resistant to repent. I fear he won't be with us much longer."

"*Jah*," Barbara near whispered. "We visited him first thing this morning."

The room spun. Gracie held onto the table.

"My dear, you're so pale," Barbara said in alarm.

"Is she going to faint?" Gideon asked his wife.

Gracie struggled to breathe. She put her head on the table and fear grew as her chest tightened. "My heart... Doc Mast."

Within fifteen minutes, Doc Mast was beside Gracie, Flora taking her pulse.

Gracie let the dam break and cried. Silas leave the Amish? Gideon apologized for upsetting her and Barbara offered Gracie a hug. They'd check on her later.

Doc Mast and Flora sat across the table from Gracie. "I don't know why I'm crying. I thought I was having a heart attack. My *daed* died of one and—"

"You're fine," Doc Mast assured. "You were having a panic attack, something I see all too much these days."

"But I'm Amish. And we live in peace…"

"Calm individuals can still experience stress buildup. During your visit I mentioned fatigue being a symptom of stress. Did Gideon or Barbara say something to upset you?"

"He told me Silas won't repent for going to your church. It was like being hit by lightning. Silas has been Amish his whole life."

Doc Mast leaned forward. "Many leave. Why do you care so much?"

Gracie ogled him. "Because he'll be shunned."

"Many are shunned."

What was Doc Mast doing? Was he taunting her?

Flora spoke up. "I guess we're wondering why you care so much. Do you love Silas? Do you have wedding plans?"

"We're courting, but if he jumps the fence, I can't marry him."

Doc Mast slid closer to his wife. "Flora's mother was Amish and left to be a Mennonite because of love."

Again, Gracie's head swam, and tears overflowed. "Why is everything so mixed up?"

Flora ran to her and led her to the couch. She told her husband to pick her up later. She was going to stay with Gracie until she calmed down.

Gracie felt like a child but was grateful for help. Flora offered her a glass of lemonade that was in the icebox and had some cookies on a plate. "Let's get you hydrated and get some food in you."

"Flora, what was it like for your *mamm*? How could she leave the Amish?"

Flora sat in a rocker. "Mom didn't have any regrets. She loved my *daed*. The hardest part was my *Mamm* was shunned. She got so many letters though and once I was able to read, to my shame, I read a few. Her family wrote to her regularly. And later on, I found out they met up to make quilts."

Gracie covered her mouth. "Didn't she feel guilty?"

"My mom? No. She didn't believe in shunning and was glad her family didn't abide by it."

"But they weren't following the Amish ways."

Flora pointed up. "They were following God's ways over man's ways."

Gracie repositioned the cross-stitch pillow under her head. "We should keep our word and keep our baptism vow."

Flora began rocking. "I understand the advantages of living in the Amish community. You have lots of support I wish the Mennonites could adopt. Like the auction you have once a year that brings in enough money to buy out a healthcare plan for a whole church district. I do the bills for my husband and it's either cash or very good health insurance. What we pay for our plan!" She whistled mournfully.

"Free healthcare wouldn't make me stay Amish."

"I know," Flora said. "The point I'm making is that you depend on each other more. If someone has a chimney fire, it's fixed within a day. It's amazing. We don't have that in our Mennonite church. We hire a contractor."

Gracie offered a faint smile. "Seems like your *mamm* told you stories about her Amish upbringing that you admire."

"Yes, she did. Many stories. But she loved my dad more than any Amish way of living. You need to ask yourself if you love Silas more, too."

"Flora, how old were you when you married your

husband?"

"Well, it took him twelve years of school, including his residency. We waited until he finished, so I was in my late twenties."

"*Ach,* I'm considered an old *maidel* now. I'm only twenty-seven. Between you and me, I think the Amish are backwards about spinsters. Do you know that if I don't marry soon, one of my siblings will have to build a little house off of theirs? I'm not to live here alone and need to marry."

"My goodness! The pressure you're under." Flora rose and paced. "I'd be having panic attacks if I was in your shoes, too. How much time do you need to think?"

"I don't know. Unmarried Amish women live with their parents. Mine are gone. I think everyone assumes I'm marrying Silas in November." She groaned. "He won't repent and now he's not considered marriage material." Gracie wrung her hands. "It's an unspoken pressure. *Ach,* I'm so anxious."

Flora slid the rocker closer to Gracie and plopped herself in it. "Do you know the Serenity Prayer?"

"*Jah.* God grant me the serenity to accept the things I cannot change; courage to change the things I can; and wisdom to know the difference."

"Go on. Say the whole thing," Flora said.

"That's all I know."

Flora continued the prayer. "Living one day at a time; Enjoying one moment at a time; Accepting hardships as the pathway to peace; Taking, as He did, this sinful world as it is, not as I would have it; Trusting that He will make all things right if I surrender to His Will; That I may be reasonably happy in this life and supremely happy with Him Forever in the next. Amen."

Flora glowed after saying the prayer. "You see Gracie, live one day at a time, enjoy it, and trust God to reveal his plan for you. Remember the Israelites in the wilderness? Their manna supply lasted only for a day. 'Give us this day our daily bread,' Jesus taught us to pray."

Gracie grew calmer. "I can do one day."

Flora beamed. "Yes, you can."

# Chapter 21

*Dear Gracie,*

*I heard through the grapevine you went to a Mennonite church! Bad news spreads fast! Don't let Silas tempt you to jump the fence! He's such a smooth talker.*

*Gracie, I'm worried about you! You've been tired and now maybe you're too tired to think straight. Can you come down here again? You know you're always welcome.*

*Luke*

∞∞∞

*Dear Luke,*

*Remember how we'd examine bugs with a magnifying glass? Well, that's how I feel right now. I'm upset and lacking Gelassenheit. I must yield myself to the church ministers, but it's harder than I thought. I saw nothing wrong with the Mennonite service. It reminded me of the deep talks we'd have about the Bible as a family.*

*Silas is not a smooth talker, Luke. He's having some kind of spiritual awakening. Do you know their family didn't study the Bible like our family? Deacon Gideon even said how Daed spoke so freely about his faith that it made him uncomfortable.*

*This is so confusing. Silas is under a temporary ban until he repents and I'm not to see him.*

*I'm sorry if my behavior has upset you. I'll be staying here though. Your fish call to you and my chickens and goats call to me. Shep is a real comfort, too.*

*Love you bruder,*

*Gracie*

∞∞∞

Gracie endured two weeks of being watched. Was it her imagination but did Amish folk she'd known her whole life seemed to look down on her. She sat that afternoon crocheting with the bold colors banned by the Amish. They used these colors in crazy quilts, so she could have a throw that was eye-popping.

Shep barked at the back door, and Gracie cringed. Not another visit from the ministers. Of course they were trying to help her. See if it was grief making her act so strange, but she just couldn't admit to it. She was concerned about Silas.

"Hello?"

She turned to see Silas. "*Ach,* you're not supposed to be here. We're being watched."

His carefree spirit was subdued. "I came to talk to you. If someone reports it, I'll take all the blame."

Gracie tapped the rocker next to her. "Sit down."

Silas fiddled his fingers for a spell. A red-tailed hawk screeched. And Shep seemed to stare through Silas. "I need to tell you something, Gracie. Ask you, I suppose." He sighed. "We're going to leave the Amish. My whole family."

She spun towards him. "Silas, I told you to be careful. You got to close to the fire!"

He got up, hands shoved in his pockets. "Gracie, we believe like they do. Why all these walls among the Amish? It's fear and God hasn't given us a spirit of fear, but power, love, and a sound mind. That's in the Bible and I refuse to be intimidated anymore with manmade rules."

Gracie squeezed her yarn, ready to choke it. "You'd leave after Menno mentored you, the People helped you fix your house, get a veal farm going? Where's your gratitude? "

He slouched. "I do feel bad about that. We hope to pay back the Gmay when possible. We just can't live under such rules."

"My *Mamm* and *Daed* explained rules keep us safe, like guard rails along the road. Keeps us from getting hurt and keeps us brave. Would you cross Cherry Creek River with no rails on the side?"

He forced a smile. "I suppose I would."

His look of innocence was so endearing she wanted to hold him. Wanted to keep him safe within the Amish community. "Well, as mad as I am about how I'm being treated, I can't leave the Amish. The good outweighs the bad, and Silas, we both made a vow to the church, one that's as strong as a marriage vow. How can you break it?"

He knelt before her. "Gracie, I still want you to marry me."

She touched his face, surprised at the emotion that overcame her. "Silas, I can't leave the People."

He kissed her hand. "How about we move to a less strict Amish group? There's plenty in Ohio."

She searched his eyes. Silas truly loved her. No hint of lust but genuine love. "*Ach,* Silas, stay here and repent. Stay away from the Mennonites. Many people have the new birth you mentioned."

To her shock, he pulled her out of her rocker, her hot pink yarn falling to the floor. "I love you. Please, leave with me." He stroked her cheek and kissed her ever so gently. "I'll stay Amish if we find a settlement that's not so strict."

She leaned her head on his shoulder. "I hear there's New Order Amish out in Indiana, but it's so far away."

"We'd be together…"

She met his gaze and they fell into a mutual kiss, ignoring Shep barking to beat the band. They ignored the kitchen screen door squeaking open, until they heard William's voice.

"What's going on?" William roared. "Silas, you're not supposed to be talking to Gracie."

He smiled. "I think she just agreed to be my wife."

∞∞∞

The next day, a driver dropped off her twin at her place. Teresa, Rachel and Bruce were already there. Gracie didn't offer any cookies or coffee, since she didn't plan this meeting. She sat in her rocker, Shep at her feet and crocheted her 'crazy blanket'.

As soon as she saw Luke, her heart melted. He looked like he hadn't slept and knew he'd been crying. "Gracie, I'm taking you home to Smicksburg," he blurted. "If you're shunned, I'll lose my other half. Twins share a special bond."

Gracie was determined to make an adult decision,

not be treated like the little sister, but Luke disarmed her. She rose and they embraced. "I'm sorry to worry you."

"We're all worried," Rachel snapped. "Don't you care about this family?"

Luke put a hand up. "Rachel, Gracie's been the most devoted to this family, caring for *mamm* like she did." He eyed his twin. "Something else is bothering you, am I right?"

Gracie refused to admit she feared being an old *maidel*. Having to live in a small house off of Teresa and William's farm. "I have to move on. "I want what you all have - a spouse and children."

As Luke led her to the table, Teresa got up to hug her. "You have a *Mamm's* heart and of course you want marriage and a family. You're not too old to find someone special. I think Silas asking you to leave the Amish is selfish. He's only thinking about what he wants."

"He loves me," Gracie defended. "We'll just move to a less strict church district out in Indiana."

"It may as well be the moon," Bruce mumbled.

As they all sat, Luke held Gracie's hand. "What's upsetting me is that Silas wouldn't be a *gut* husband. Silas is like a yoyo. What if he changes his mind out in Indiana? He may just get you out there and jump the fence."

"So, you're saying he's deceiving me?" Gracie near shouted as tears pulled in her eyes.

"What I'm seeing is a girl afraid to be overlooked and will be an old *maidel*," Rachel scowled. "It's so obvious."

Teresa's back arched. "She could have solved that problem if she'd accepted your husband years ago!"

Bruce cackled. "That is true."

Rachel harrumphed and said Gracie chased her husband and that was that. The ridiculousness of it all made everyone burst into nervous laughter.

"Truth is, Gracie, you're too picky and now that you're old, you're desperate enough to jump the fence." Rachel squared her jaw, waiting for a retort from Gracie.

"You're right," Gracie said. "Silas has tugged at my heart since I was young. We've secretly dated for a long time, me always trying to keep him on the straight and narrow."

Luke squeezed her hand. "You deserve a mature, strong man."

"I do, but not too many around. And I care about Silas..."

"Do you love him?" Teresa pressed.

"It depends on what you call love. Long suffering like

the Bible says, *jah*, I suffered patiently with him. He's been patient with me."

Bruce steepled his fingers. "Gracie, Silas hasn't patiently waited for you. He's a flirt."

"That was in the past," Gracie said evenly. "He never saw an example of a *gut* marriage and now, he's a new man. He's so different. Can't you all see that?"

Teresa took Gracie's hand. "I see that Silas has changed. He went from atheist to believer. Of course we're all glad about that. But we grow in our Christian faith. We start out like seeds, and it takes years of watering and sunshine to mature. Are you willing to overlook Silas's faults as he grows in his newfound faith?" She looked around for help. "We all know how marriage can be a challenge at times."

Gracie listened to Teresa because she knew how much she cared.

∞∞∞

Luke and Gracie stayed up late that night, sipping lemonade on the back porch.

Luke went down memory lane, all the sights and sounds foreign to him since he moved to Smicksburg.

They laughed and then grew solemn as they shared how much they missed their parents. "We were too young to lose them both," Luke said. "Sometimes I'm jealous of Abigail having both parents to talk to."

Gracie was surprised. "You don't feel connected to her family?"

"*Jah*, I do. But there's nothing like your real kin. And sometimes I miss Cherry Creek, truth be told."

She leaned on him as they sat on the back steps, like they did as *kinner*. "You could move back here."

"*Nee*, I'm planted in Smicksburg, but sometimes I feel uprooted."

"You've made lots of *gut* friends, *jah*?"

He grinned. "Leander's like a *bruder*."

Her stomach tightened. Maryann had suggested talking to Luke about his *gut* buddy, but the words got caught in her throat. "I feel the same about Maryann and Betty."

Luke shifted. "Leander asked about you."

She gasped. "How so?"

"Well, you left right after Silas visited, not even saying good-bye."

Gracie thought back to the Mennonite service and how emotions rose while reading Psalm 23. "Leander is a *gut* shepherd, but he's not for me."

Luke wrapped his arm around his sister. "Can you

tell me you love Silas? That you've forgotten all about Leander?"

This puzzled her. Luke knew about Leah and Leander. Why was he bringing up such a painful topic? "He said he'd write, but he hasn't. He said some mighty bold things to me, so I'm not very trusting in men."

"What did he say?"

"Oh, that he'd like to be my shepherd. He asked me to write and not make a decision about Silas until I've waited."

Luke whistled a mournful tone. "He must have been smitten."

"As in past tense, not present. He played with my feelings, and I don't see that he's any different from Silas."

Luke took her by the shoulders. "*Schwester*, Leander hurt you, and you ran back to Silas."

By the full moon, Gracie saw her twin's torment over her, and she broke down and sobbed, leaning her head on his shoulder. "*Jah*, he hurt me."

He rocked her a bit and she let out pent up sorrow. "I wish I never met him."

Luke held her until she was wrung out. "*Danki* for being here." She drew out a tissue from her pocket. "I got some *gut* advice from a friend. A Mennonite friend. She can recite the whole Serenity Prayer. The one that tells us to accept the things we cannot change, change the things we can and the wisdom to know the difference."

He nodded. "I like that. Go on."

"Well, I never heard the whole prayer. It says at least twice to take each day as it comes. Flora encouraged me to just live one day and it calmed me down. Thinking of my whole life is daunting, but one day I can do. Flora also said I'm not an old *maidel*. She got married when she was in her late twenties, and I got to thinking. My neighbor got married in her thirties and I think the Amish push too much for young marriages."

Luke grabbed his straw hat and fanned his face. "That sounds like something the English would say…"

"*Jah*, it does, but for me, it takes the pressure off. Like I said, I can do one day. So, I'll tell Silas that I can't marry him until I have no doubts."

"Phew. I'm glad you have doubts. I don't see you with him."

"I'll humble myself and live under the Amish rule. Unmarried women don't live alone. I'll live in a little house off of Teresa and Williams."

"What?" Luke groaned. "Gracie, come live with me."

She hugged him. "Danki, but I need my space. I'd be

a nuisance. Two women in the kitchen never worked too *gut*."

A squirrel scurried up a tree. A barn owl hooted.

"It's because of Leander," Luke said with a moan. "Something's mixed up between you two. I know he cares for you."

"And Leah, too?"

Luke pulled at his beard. "I have to admit, I've seen them together. But Leander isn't deceitful. Do you want me to talk to him?"

"What's there to say?" Gracie felt her face flush and feared another anxiety attack.

"Leander thinks you went back to Cherry Creek because of Silas. Folks in our area saw Silas and the girls spread rumors he's so handsome and all that nonsense." Luke sat erect and snapped his fingers. "That's it. Deep down Leander must be self-conscious of his birthmark, and now all the scars."

"How bad is it?"

"Would you care, Gracie?"

"Nee. I'm not shallow. But I don't want you to give him hope. Even if I left Smicksburg because of Silas, why didn't he write like he promised. I know he's recovered." She hugged herself. "I want someone who truly loves me. Someone who will pursue me. Not someone I have to encourage."

Luke put an arm around his sister. "You're being too hard on Leander, but I won't say anything. Now, fill me in on your plans."

"Well, I'll sell the house—"

"For a million dollars?"

"*Nee,* much less. William can afford less than half that amount. But, he'd be selling his place, so I don't know."

"Do the others know about this?" Luke asked, his tone flat.

"Do I have to ask permission? The house is mine, *jah*?"

He held up his hand. "Believe me, let's talk to the others tomorrow."

# Chapter 22

Early the next morning, while Gracie was having her morning coffee, watching the sunrise, a buggy pulled in. Silas! He near skipped to the side of the house and let himself in as was their custom.

"Good morning, my bride to be," he said, kissing her cheek. "I have news." He poured himself some coffee and sat next to her, taking a sticky bun from the plate on the table. Since Gracie was silent, he eyed her. "Are you okay? Doc Mast told me about your panic attack. I wanted to come yesterday but saw so many buggies. Who came over?"

She put a finger to her lips. "Not so loud. You'll wake up Luke."

"He's here?" Silas scowled. "To talk you out of marrying me."

"He's concerned. Word got out that I was going to marry you and all my siblings came yesterday."

"And they talked you out of it?"

His puppy dog eyes pulled at her heart. "They have concerns about me being shunned. It is a big step."

He took her hands. "They bully you around. You're a grown woman who can decide on her own."

Gracie inhaled. "I've decided not to decide. We talked about courting until November." She squeezed his hands. "Maybe I'll know by then."

His eyes grew round. "But I'm leaving. My whole family is moving to Ohio."

"We can write?"

He slouched in his chair. "You'll forget all about me, just like you forgot me when you lived with your *bruder*."

"Alice took your letters, remember?"

"My *dochder* did what?" Luke near boomed behind them. "Gracie, Silas is shunned. Silas, leave this house. Don't you care about Gracie's reputation? Or Amish rules?"

Silas kept his cool. "Those rules were made by man, not God."

"Leave," Luke said firmly, pointing to the door.

To Gracie's shock, he meekly walked to the door to leave. She ran to him. "Silas, I'll need to know your address."

He offered a faint smile. "I'll write first."

She nodded in consent and then turned to face her brother. "You were rude."

Luke's brows knit together. "I was rude? Jesus flipped over tables! I was nice! Gracie, he's shunned. You can't talk or write to him."

Gracie said nothing, but bowed her head, shooting up a prayer for help.

∞∞∞

By noon, all the siblings were sharing a picnic basket, seated on a vast blanket. Gracie picked at her food, having no appetite, even though Teresa made a feast.

"This was a *gut* idea, Luke. To see you before you go back home," Teresa beamed.

"Well, we have something to talk about." He glanced at Gracie to see if she'd start the conversation, but she didn't. "Well, this house will be sold."

Rachel held her heart. "Gracie, are you leaving with Silas? Going to Ohio?"

Teresa gripped Gracie's wrist. "My little *schwester* go to Ohio with Silas?"

"*Nee,* I'm not. Silas and his family are moving."

Luke spoke up. "Gracie isn't going with him. But she

wants to sell the house to you, Teresa and William."

"*Jah*, we've talked about that," William said.

Rachel clawed in. "For a million bucks?"

Luke gawked. "*Nee,* not even half a million."

"But that's what it's worth," Rachel glowered

"I'd give the house to William and Teresa, if I had my way." Gracie explained.

Rachel choked on her sandwich. Her husband hit her back until she shooed him away, saying she was fine. "Gracie, you can't make that decision."

"The house was left to me," Gracie was surprised at her confident tone. "And since I've decided not to marry—"

"Be an old *maidel!*" Rachel screamed.

"I'm not old. Many outside the Amish marry much older. But, anyway, until I'm sure God's brought me the right man, I won't marry. Our strict rules have hemmed me in, but I will submit, since I believe I'm Amish to my core."

Quiet hung in the air like clouds.

"I'm so proud of you," Teresa gushed. "You could have settled for someone long ago."

Gracie let the comment pass. She'd be writing Silas and if he returned to the flock, they'd wed.

"Do you expect God to have your husband fall from the sky?" Bruce asked, rather gruffy.

"You know what she means," Luke defended. "She's taking one day at a time. Gracie wants God's will for her life and she's taking it day by day. Now, loosen up. We're family and you know Gracie's been under too much stress. No wonder she needs time to think."

They fell back into harmony, but the question about the house being sold Rachel quickly brought up. "Why isn't the house being sold for the going price?"

"To keep it in the family!" Bruce boomed. "I'm fine with that. *Daed* and *Mamm* never acted money hungry, and neither should we. I say we let William and Teresa buy it."

Despite Rachel's protest, they took a vote, and it was decided that the house would stay in the family. Rachel stood, arms akimbo. She demanded Gideon, the deacon, have a say-so. No one agreed to this because it was a family matter, not a church concern. Gracie was being generous to share any of the profit of the homestead.

Rachel motioned for her husband, Jeremiah, to get up. "We're leaving."

To her astonishment, he told her to sit herself back down and treat her siblings with respect. Gracie wanted to applaud. Rachel plopped down but crossed her arms in defiance.

William offered to build a small house on the

property for Gracie, but Bruce suggested they fix up the *dawdyhaus* back in the woods. It was run down, but they could have it livable in no time. Gracie didn't know the *dawdyhaus* could be repaired and was tickled beyond belief at the possibility. She'd have the woods and tiny creek that trickled nearby to relax her. A perfect quiet place to heal. And, how she needed it.

∞ ∞ ∞

Over the next week, work crews gutted out the tiny house, tore off the front porch, replaced plumbing and a yard appeared as women mowed, weeded, and even planted a few rose bushes. Gracie had talked so much about the wise woman, Granny Weaver, and her small house surrounded by roses.

Gracie hugged Maryann and Betty. "I wonder who bought the roses."

"Not me," they said in unison.

"Maybe Granny Weaver," Maryann said. "I'd like to meet her sometime. We should take a ride down and stay a few days."

Gracie stiffened. "*Nee,* I don't want to go to Smicksburg anytime soon."

Betty rubbed Gracie's back. "What is it? Are you

245

upset with Luke? About how he treated Silas?"

The two friends could read her, so she asked if they could take a walk behind the house. "My *opa* made this path. Seeing the house torn down makes me sad. Miss my grandparents."

Maryann looped her arm through Gracie's. "Someone's trying to change the subject. Why don't you want to go to Smicksburg? I'd love to go to that yarn shop."

Gracie knew she could trust these two to keep her secret. "You two think I'll be single, *jah*?"

"The whole town does," Betty whispered.

"This needs to stay between us. I think I experienced actual love with Leander. But I can't have him, so I'll remain single until by some miracle there's another man like him out there that's Amish."

Maryann pat Gracie's back. "You finally said it. What's been bottled up in that heart of yours is pretty sad. A heavy load. Can't you talk to Leander?"

"He said he'd write but never has. Luke has seen him with Leah."

Betty kicked a stone down the path. "Maybe it's all a mix up. If Leander is the man you say he is, would he be deceitful?"

"We can deceive ourselves, I suppose," Gracie said. "Luke said that when Silas came to visit, it got all over

Smicksburg what a handsome man I'm engaged to. Leander's sore that I never said goodbye, too."

The three sat on a log near the creek. All was quiet. Too quiet.

Gracie glanced at her friends. "Did I say something wrong?"

"Just thinking," Betty said. "Do you think Leander is comparing himself to Silas? Does he feel he's not *gut* enough for you?"

"That's silly."

Maryann cleared her throat. "Not for someone who thinks they're the ugly duckling. I never let on how ugly I felt compared to my *schwestern*, remember?"

"But Leander is so handsome," Gracie said with a sigh. "How can he think he's ugly?"

"He's got a port wine stain, *jah*?" Betty asked. "Did he get teased while young?"

Gracie stared through the thick woods across the creek. "*Jah*, he did. Luke told me he's dated plenty but always breaks things off so he can reject first before he can be rejected."

"That's so sad," Maryann near pouted. "I feel for him. It'll take lots of love for him to overcome that."

Betty made Gracie look at her. "How do you feel about yourself? Silas has been teasing you for how long? Has he guilt tripped you? You seem too...."

"Responsible for his happiness. Or for him to be a *gut* man?" Maryann prodded.

"He is a *gut* man now," Gracie said.

"Let me ask another question," Betty said. "Does Leander need any changing?"

Her friends' probing questions dislodged her defenses. Was she having an epiphany? She felt like layers were being peeled back. Yes, she thought she could change Silas. So many moments together flashed through her mind. Yes, she wanted to change him. *Am I too compassionate, like Granny Weaver said?*

She picked up a stone and flung it into the creek. "I wouldn't change anything about Leander. He's not perfect, but he's not wild, like Silas used to be."

"And still is," Maryann said. "He's a yoyo. Asks you to marry him, leave the Amish for a liberal group in Ohio. I'm sorry, Gracie. I couldn't live with a moody man like that. He's…immature."

Gracie hung her head, deep in thought. *Faithful are the wounds of a friend*, it said in Proverbs. They were speaking out of love and concern.

"Gracie, are we being too hard on you?" Maryann near whispered.

"*Nee,* I appreciate your honesty. We all have blind spots, *jah?*"

"Gut, because I have another question. Gracie, you're

the prettiest girl in town. How come you turned down every marriage proposal?"

"I didn't love any of them..."

"Did you get to know any of them? Have you ever had a long courtship?"

"Nee. Well, almost. With Johnny Kline when I was eighteen. He scared me," Gracie said. "We courted for six months, but I think I was too young. I've always felt that it's too much pressure to plan your whole life when a teenager. But you two have helped me. I think I've felt responsible for Silas' happiness. His faithfulness to the Amish church."

"How did that happen?" Maryann asked.

"Because he told me I kept him on the straight and narrow. That I made him happy."

Betty slid next to Gracie and leaned her head on Gracie's shoulder. "You're too nice, is what. That's a heavy burden for anyone to bear. Only God can keep Silas from falling. Only God can give Silas true contentment and happiness."

It was as if a wet blanket was lifted off of Gracie. "Maybe that's why I felt so free around Leander. He doesn't have any baggage."

"I'm sure he's not perfect, Maryann said. "We all have our crosses to bear." She appeared hesitant to continue, but said, "Gracie, you said Leander broke things off with girls so he wouldn't be rejected first. Maybe he appears to be rejecting you but he hasn't. He's just protecting his heart."

"And you're protecting yours," Betty said.

The three leaned into each other. *A cord of three strands is not easily broken.* Gracie would be leaning on these friends while living in the *dawdyhaus*. She would live under the shadow of the Almighty. She would trust her Good Shepherd to lead.

# Chapter 23

*D*ear Luke,
    *A few days ago, Gracie told me she had an epiphany of sorts. She's done with Silas. I'm RELIEVED! He did nothing wrong, Gracie said. She doesn't have a smidgen of hopelessness, though. I've never seen her so carefree. According to her, she made attempts to keep Silas on the right path, but it left her feeling drained.*

*Gracie mentioned that if there were another man like your friend, Leander, she would possibly consider marriage. She's convinced he's taken. Gracie also has been influenced by Outsiders that Amish marry too young, and she'll wait until she's in her thirties.*

*The dawdyhaus is coming along. It's amazing how fast it has been transformed. Gracie will move in next week. It was good of you to send the rose bushes. They're mature enough to plant now. Gracie's Mennonite friend, Flora, has heirloom roses and is going to help Gracie care for them.*

*Rachel's newborn is doing good. Gracie is going to help*

*her over the next few days. She wants to build a bridge to our prickly sister. I have to say, I'm mighty proud of my twins. Since Mamm passed, I feel like a mother hen looking over the youngest.*

*Love you bruder,*

*Teresa*

Luke let the letter fall onto the table. "Abigail, did you send Gracie roses?"

Her brows lifted as she sipped her morning coffee. "Why would I send Gracie roses?"

Luke scratched the back of his neck. "This doesn't make sense. Someone sent mature rose bushes to go around Gracie's little house."

"Granny Weaver loves roses. Maybe she sent them."

"It would be expensive. I hope Silas didn't send them. *Ach,* I'm relieved she put an end to their relationship, but he has a way of wiggling into Gracie's heart."

Abigail smiled. "You're not awake. Let me read the letter. I know nothing about her breaking things off."

Abigail read the brief letter and her eyes twinkled. "Her eyes have been open. Silas has no wiggle room in Gracie's heart."

"How do you know that?"

She cupped Luke's hand. "Experience. There were things about Allen I tried to fix. When I met you, I met a strong man. One I could respect."

He kissed her hand. "I love you, Abigail Hershberger."

She hugged him. And I love you. Now, what's on your calendar today?"

"The fish are calling to me, but I'd rather have a day with my girl."

"Alice is over at Jenny's," she teased, poking him.

"Abigail, you're the best tonic I've got. Let's ditch any plans and I'll court you today."

She held her cheeks in astonishment and then kissed her husband but *gut*.

∞∞∞

The next day, Luke and Leander drove to Keystone Lake, a canoe hitched up to their buggy. Lots of people who passed by stopped and tried to get a picture, but Luke didn't care right now. He had Gracie on his mind. Silas sent her roses and will worm his way back into her heart.

Leander seemed as glum as he felt, but he supposed he was still grieving the loss of his brother. Storm clouds appeared over the mountain and Luke groaned. "We should pull into Silver Canoe. I don't want to get drenched."

Leander agreed, adding that he wanted to buy some snacks. "*Mamm* packs me an entire meal when I come down here but forgot. I could do it myself, but she enjoys taking care of me. *Mamm*'s not herself, but—"

"But what?"

"*Ach,* it's nothing. Let's get something to eat."

They ordered hamburgers and fries and sat at one of the outside tables, monitoring the clouds. Maybe they would just pass.

"Your *mamm* has looked so tired. Does she need help?"

Leander twisted up his lips. "I'm not supposed to tell anyone, but I've kept this thing in too long. Promise you won't tell anyone?"

"*Nee,* I can't. What if it's something that the church elders need to know?"

"Nothing like that. It's a personal thing."

"Go on."

"Well, Leah was going to court Hezekiah when he returned. They courted in secret when they were younger. They wrote and were planning on getting married."

Luke shook his head in disbelief. "But, didn't you court her?"

"For a short time. She kept asking if my port wine

stain was hereditary. I broke it off. It was only a few months before I knew she wasn't for me, anyhow."

"Did she ever ask Hezekiah about birthmarks?"

"Hezekiah didn't have any. We've had long talks and she apologized to me for making me feel self-conscious. And then she started to care for me. I knew she was in shock and grief, but I never led her on. I was only her friend."

"Don't you care for her at all?"

"*Nee,* and *Mamm* is upset. We can only be *gut* friends."

"Why is that?" Luke asked, hoping to get Leander to admit he still cared for Gracie.

Leander's eyes deadened. "I can't have the girl I want."

"And that would be?"

Leander grew irritated. "You know who. Gracie never said goodbye and is off with that man who doesn't deserve her."

Luke jumped up and fist pumped the air. "Praise be!!"

Leander's mouth gaped. "What is wrong with you?"

"Did you send rose bushes to Gracie? Please tell me that you did. Because she dumped Silas and I'm afraid he sent them, and he might worm his way into her heart." He inhaled, out of breath. "I'm so worried about her. I know she loves you."

"Why would I send roses? What! She's done with Silas? I thought they were getting married."

Luke let out a laugh. "*Nee,* they are not."

"Jeb Weaver said they're building a house."

"It's a *dawdyhaus.* Gracie said she'd be an old *maidel* before she married someone she didn't love."

Leander's eyes misted. "A *dawdyhaus*? So she's single…"

"She said she can't have the man she loves because he's already taken."

Leander reddened. "Who's that?"

Luke slapped Leander's back. "I can't tell anyone."

"Is he from Cherry Creek?"

Luke pretended to ponder. "*Nee,* not from New York."

Leander's eyes grew round. "She can't mean me."

"Hey goofy, I said I can't tell you but I'm kind of spelling it out."

Leander removed his straw hat. "She wouldn't want a face like this." He grew too solemn. "I'm afraid."

Luke shot up a prayer for wisdom. "Afraid. Fear of rejection. It keeps you in chains. If you love Gracie, go visit her."

"She's a beauty who deserves better."

Luke thought of a proverb his parents always said. "Buddy, Courage is fear that has said its prayers. Get on your knees and get out of that pit."

∞ ∞ ∞

*Dear Gracie,*

*I hope you like the rose bushes I sent. Flora arranged it all. Did you guess it was me?*

*I hope you're praying about our future together. There are New Order Amish settlements all over the place here in Ohio. I love driving a car but would give that up for you. No cars allowed with the New Order.*

*I got a job at an RV manufacturer. It's fast-paced but I don't mind it. When we can afford land, Daed wants to farm and raise veal again.*

*Sorry this is so short. I'm writing it on my work break.*

*I love you Gracie,*

*Silas*

∞ ∞ ∞

*Dear Granny Weaver,*

*I miss you. I miss your advice so I'm writing this letter. I hope you are well.*

*Maybe you've heard, but I'm living in the dawdyhaus behind my sister. Teresa and her family moved into the family homestead. I'm feeling more settled, but I need to let Silas know I can't leave the Amish. Actually, I have to tell him I can't marry him. I don't love him. I've cared for him as a friend since we were kinner and felt sorry for him. His upbringing was rough. Truth be told, I'm living in this dawdyhaus because I will not marry Silas and I think the pressure to marry is too young among the Amish.*

*Here's my question. How can I tell Silas I can't marry him? I don't want to hurt him.*

*Any advice is appreciated.*

*I send a big hug with this short note,*
*Gracie Hershberger*

Teresa and William read Luke's letter. "I like the plan. But how do we get Gracie to go?"

Teresa swooshed her hand. "Women like auctions. And it's for a *gut* cause. Now, I'll get Gracie to think of things she wants for her hope chest."

Michael groaned. "She has hope?"

"She will when she sees him at the auction. I just know they'll see each other, like we did, and just know they're the right one for each other."

Michael pulled Teresa on his lap. "I'm so glad I found

you. We'll have to help Luke with his plan. What day is it?"

"The first Saturday of the month. So, we'll go on July 6th. That's in two weeks." She hugged her husband. "I'm so glad I have my best friend with me here in Cherry Creek." She kissed his cheek. "I have a feeling my twin siblings will be living in Smicksburg."

*Dear Gracie,*

*I've been praying for you and am happy with your decision to stay Amish. Once you decide, everything seems to fall into place. I was engaged to a man who jumped the fence and turned Mennonite, so I do feel for you and Silas. I told my old beau, and he didn't give up chasing me, but when I found Jeb, I knew he was what God intended for me. You see, Gracie, as much as I call myself a matchmaker, I pray and let the Good Lord match people up. I introduce and help them see each other's good qualities.*

*I think there is someone out there who is divinely appointed to you. You just have to wait. Waiting is something we do most of our lives. And then when we get what we're waiting for, we need to wait for something*

*else. So, it's good to practice waiting.*
   *Love,*
   *Granny Weaver*

∞∞∞

Gracie relished living alone in her cozy little house. The interior was a pale mint green and it soothed her. She felt content for the first time in ages. Writing to Silas several days ago was so hard, but necessary. She hoped they could talk face to face, but being Amish, letters had to do, even for important matters.

She sipped apple cider and dreamed about her future plans. Starting a fabric store with Teresa seemed ideal, but she wanted to be more independent. Hold down a job apart from her family. Deacon Gideon had mentioned teaching in one of the schools come fall, and she'd probably accept.

Shep's ears perked up and then his low growl rumbled. Gracie heard a car and figured it was a driver for Teresa or William, but the car continued on to her house. She pulled back the white curtain and gasped. Silas!

She ran to meet him on her little porch. "Silas, I was hoping we could talk. A letter was so impersonal."

"*Jah*, Gracie. Can I come in, even though I'm shunned?"

Gracie said she had lawn chairs behind the house overlooking the creek, and they could talk there. She hoped no one would see them and was a smidgen nervous. But, Silas deserved this talk.

After they took their seats, Silas leaned forward and fidgeted with his fingers. "Gracie, I've met so many people in Holmes County. It's gigantic compared to Cherry Creek and I've met so many people. I never knew how isolated I was here."

Gracie watched Silas' face closely. He had something painful to say. "What is it, Silas? Did you drive back here to return to the People or to see me?"

"Well, I'm picking up the Micah Miller family. They're jumping the fence, too."

Gracie blinked in disbelief. "But Micah is one of the ministers."

"And he thinks he needs to do just that. Minister to people freely, not with so many rules."

Gracie felt herself grow limp. "*Ach*, I'm in shock."

"Gracie, do you realize how isolated Cherry Creek Amish are? I've made many new friends in a short time."

Gracie cocked her head. "You've met someone, haven't you?"

He blushed. "I'm sorry, Gracie. No one special, but one girl makes me feel I've known her for years."

Gracie thought of Leander. "I know what you mean, and I'm happy for you. Maybe we tricked ourselves into thinking we should get married since we were told that since teenagers."

He reached for her hand, and she took it. "No hard feelings?"

"No hard feelings. I'll miss you. You're so…"

"Familiar?"

"*Jah*, I'm used to having you around. I love you as a friend and don't want to lose touch. Will you write?"

"But I'm shunned," he said, appearing confused.

"Not long letters. Maybe a postcard from Holmes County from time to time so I know how you and your family are doing."

They squeezed each other's hands in agreement.

# Chapter 24

Teresa leaned toward Gracie. "It's so nice to celebrate *Schwester* Day, don't you think, Rachel?"

Rachel nodded. "I don't know if I should have come since I'm ready to give birth. *Ach,* and the heat in Pennsylvania is going to kill me."

Gracie smirked. "Rachel, remember how we're going to look for the sunny side of life?"

Rachel nodded. "Sorry, but I'm so squished in this van."

"At least there's air conditioning," Teresa pointed out. "Such a muggy, hot day."

Rachel tapped Gracie's shoulder. "I'm going to try, you know. Give more gratitude and thanks. Not see my cup half empty all the time."

Teresa gazed in disbelief. "What are you talking about?"

"Gracie has been helping me around the house since I'm huge with child, and we talked about how her being a chipper songbird grates on my nerves. She's one of those fancy mockingbirds who show off all their songs and dances, while I'm just a plain robin."

"Did you say mockingbird?" Gracie asked in astonishment.

"*Jah*, I did."

"Danki. I was so depressed when *Mamm* died, I saw a mockingbird dancing and singing and asked the Lord to make me like that bird. How odd you'd say that."

"You don't see yourself that way?" Teresa asked.

"Nee. Well, I was mighty sad, but I know how much I fret and fear things. Isn't that part of being human?"

"*Jah*, it is," Teresa said. "But you and Luke have always seemed so carefree."

Gracie considered this. "I've tried to be like *Mamm*. She was the true songbird."

"She rubbed off on you," Rachel said. "*Oma* Hershberger rubbed off on me. She could be a crank."

The three sisters giggled. "She was," Teresa admitted.

"I barely remember her, being too young," Gracie said.

"Really?" Teresa asked. "That's too bad. She wasn't a crank all the time. She was just straightforward, like I am at times."

"You're the most like *Daed*," Gracie said. "He just

oozed peace. He really trusted God. Had great faith and seemed to know God had everything under control."

The three clasped hands. "I'm glad I have you two for *schwestern* ," Rachel said.

Gracie was so surprised, she hugged Rachel. "I'm so glad we had time to talk over these past few weeks. And when the *boppli* comes, I'll be over to help. I have so much free time being single."

∞∞∞

Gracie, Teresa and Rachel pinned a white wedding ring quilt to the clothesline. They stepped back to admire it. All the stitches so tiny and even, made to support the local Amish medical aid. They'd plan to make another one for their auction in August.

"The Hershberger *schwestern* learned to quilt from their *Mamm*, I hear," a familiar voice chimed.

They turned to see Luke, Abigail and Alice.

Alice charged her Aunt Gracie. "I've missed you!" She then hugged her other aunts.

"Why didn't you tell us you were coming?" Gracie asked.

Alice attempted to talk, but Teresa put a hand over

her lips. "We wrote and said we might come, *jah*?"

"*Jah*," Abigail said. "We've been talking about it quite often."

Gracie scanned the growing crowd for other Smicksburg friends but didn't see any. "So, you hired a driver just for your family?"

Alice started to say something, but Teresa took her by the hand. "Let's get some lemonade."

"Granny Weaver made the lemonade," Alice chirped. "Everything she makes is yummy."

Gracie frowned. "Did she say Granny?"

"Granny and Jeb are here, along with others from our *Gmay*." Abigail said. "The knitting circle made a thick blanket that will help relieve anxiety."

Gracie's heart leapt. "Where are they?"

Luke shrugged. "Thousand or so people here, but she has a lavender dress on, so maybe you can spot her." He nodded to Abigail. "We need to set up our table. Made a few rockers. Not much, but the Smicksburg folk are sharing a booth."

They turned to leave. Gracie gawked. Luke didn't invite her to join them. Neither did her *schwestern*. Should she follow them? With everyone now out of sight among the throng, Gracie decided to sit at one of the picnic tables under the large red and white tent. She looked around for familiar faces but didn't recognize anyone. After a spell, she meandered her way through the many displays, admiring the talent among the Amish. One man had clocks and she thought of her *daed's* carving abilities. No one could carve animals like him. She was glad Teresa insisted she take the squirrel and acorn cuckoo clock.

Gracie then went into a large barn full of quilts. She'd never seen some of these patterns and wondered just how far away people came to make this auction possible. She eyed a lovely quilt in shades of purple. And Amish woman came near her. "Do you like it?"

Gracie nodded. "Did you make it?"

"*Jah*. I did it with my quilting circle out in Lancaster." She turned to point at her heart-shaped kapp, typical of Lancaster Amish.

"How far have some of the people come? I see all sorts of men's hats I've never seen before. Some *kapps* are different, too."

"Well, many of us have kin in these parts and want to help. I hear some have chartered a bus from Missouri."

Gracie felt naïve, and Silas' words about being too isolated in Cherry Creek crept into her mind. She shrugged them off though, told the Amish woman she'd bid on the quilt if she had the money and continued to admire rows and rows of quilts. Getting thirsty, she exited the building and tried to find

Granny's lemonade.

"*Ach,* honey girl," Granny quipped, running to her, giving her a hug. "I've missed you. Have you seen Luke?"

Jeb tapped his hat. "Alice has been chattering non-stop in the van about her Aunt Gracie. Wanted to put cotton in my ears."

Gracie soaked in the presence of these two sweet people. "It's so *gut* to see you again." Her eyes brimmed with tears. "*Ach,* I didn't realize how much I missed you."

Granny took her hand. "We need to catch up, but Jeb and I have to help over at the Smicksburg booth."

They too went off, leaving Gracie completely baffled. She ran after them. "I can help with your booth. I already hung a quilt we made in Cherry Creek."

Jeb pulled at his beard, looking at his feet. Granny told Jeb to go, and she'd catch up.

Granny took Gracie's hand. "Let's take a walk."

"A walk? Ah, where do you want to go?"

"To the pie section, for sure. I want to see all the possibilities to decorate a pie. I can do a lattice top but want some new ideas."

As they strolled over to the pies, Granny kept looking back.

"Do you want to ask Jeb to join us?"

"Jeb? He left."

Gracie wondered if the heat was confusing her. "Granny, everyone's acting so...peculiar."

Granny smiled. "The *gut* Lord said we'd be a peculiar people."

Feeling overwhelmed, Gracie strolled over to the nearest folding chair. "I don't feel right. I'm confused."

Granny snapped her fingers. "A lemonade is just the thing." Granny raised her hand and waved. "I see someone I know who will bring us a lemonade."

Gracie took her laced trimmed handkerchief from her pocket and wiped the perspiration from her face. "It's usually cooler in the valley."

Granny pointed to a large willow tree by a pond. "How about you go sit under the tree and I'll get your lemonade."

"But isn't someone else getting it?"

"You go on down. Isn't this a delightful farm? Such a nice spot under the willow for you to sit."

Gracie strolled down the hill, taking in the breeze the closer she got to the pond. She noticed how meticulous the grass was cut and she wondered how long it took the owner of this farm to prepare for such a huge event. When she got to the pond, she decided to stick her feet in the water, thinking it would calm her. How could Luke walk away from her? An emptiness enveloped her. He was distracted by all the activities, too, and wanted to spend time with Abigail.

She closed her eyes. *Lord, if I'm going to walk this life alone, without a spouse, please be near me. Maryann is still talking about the new family in town with five brothers in their twenties, all bachelors. How unusual. Do you have someone else for me? Someone I don't know?*

"Here's your lemonade," a deep voice said.

Gracie turned to see Leander, holding a cup to her. Her heart throbbed, and she found it difficult to compose herself.

"Gracie! I didn't know you were here!"

Blinking in disbelief, Gracie took the cup. "My, ah, *schwestern* and I came down. We're celebrating *Schwestern* Day, but I can't seem to find them..."

Leander sat next to her. "So, this is why everyone's acting so *ferhoodled*." He grinned. "I think your *bruder* and Granny Weaver arranged for us to meet."

She looked into the lake, hoping the ripples could calm her. They sat for a spell in silence. A blue heron swooped down and lowered its beak to catch a fish. Canada Geese flew overhead in their V-shaped pattern.

"They're exercising for migration," Leander near whispered.

"*Jah*, it's amazing how they take turns being in the

front, taking the brunt of the wind."

Silence again.

Gracie glanced at Leander. "How are you? Back to normal?"

He nodded. "Just more scars on this beat up face. But I'm thankful. No liver transplant and no more hospital stays, although I go to physical therapy still."

Gracie felt like she had rocks in her mouth. She was glad to be seated since she felt faint.

"I can do exercises on the farm, but they know which muscle to work." He glanced at her. "How have you been? Luke tells me you broke things off with Silas."

Gracie straightened. "*Jah*, I did."

Leander slid a bit closer. "Why?"

Irritated that he was flirting with her while seeing Leah annoyed her. "How's Leah?"

"She's plenty down."

"Oh?"

"*Jah*, she took my *brud*er's death real hard. They were engaged. She loved him."

"*Ach,* that's so sad. I thought you were—"

"Courting her. Luke told me. She needed a friend and so did I. My family has had a hard loss."

Gracie put a hand on him. "I'm so sorry. Does the pain ever ease up?"

He groaned. "I'd take physical pain anytime over

heartache. But I believe he's with the Lord, and it was His plan."

"So you're more at peace?"

Their eyes locked. She stared at the large scar on his cheek, but quickly met his eyes again.

"I'm pretty beat up, huh?"

She wanted to hold him. She yearned to be near him. "Leander, your scars don't matter to me. They aren't that bad…"

His eyes brimmed. "You only see the *gut* in people, just like Luke said. You overlooked Silas' bad behavior and now my…ugly face."

She hugged him. "You're not ugly at all." The dam within burst and she wept on his shoulder. "I can't bear for you to think you're ugly. You're handsome inside and out."

He held her at shoulder length, studying her. "Are you serious?"

Too choked up to speak further, she nodded.

"So, I still have a chance with you."

She nodded rapidly with eager eyes.

"Gracie, could you marry me?"

She flung herself on him, sobbing. "*Jah.* I love you ever so much."

When Gracie blinked back enough tears to see, she eyed Luke, Abigail, and Alice waving at the top of the hill. Alice ran down full speed.

"Aunt Gracie, did you say yes?"

"*Jah*, I did."

Alice hugged her middle. "I'm so glad you picked Leander. Yippy!" She ran back up the hill, shouting, "Gracie and Leander are getting married. For sure. Aunt Gracie's never looked so happy! Silas was getting nice, but Leander is better for my aunt."

Everyone laughed. Gracie snuggled next to Leander, and with not one doubt in her mind, she finally found someone to love.

# *Epilogue*

Gracie & Leander decided to write love letters to each other and visit until wedding season. Leander got to see the wonders of Cherry Creek, being sensitive to his bride to be that she was attached to the area. Leander was such *wunderbar gut* medicine to Rachel, him helping her with internal scars while he talked of his outward ones.

On Thanksgiving, they exchanged wedding vows at the Hershberger homestead, Teresa being a gracious host. The clocks all cuckooed and chimed after the ceremony and giggles bounced around the crowded room.

Gracie had formed a relationship with Leah, trying to help her with the loss of Hezekiah, and she was her bride's maid attendant. The two ended up becoming fast sister friends.

Through much prayer, Gracie and Leander decided to move to Smicksburg, living in a dawdyhaus until they could break land on their new house in the spring. Luke was beyond thrilled that his twin moved to Smicksburg and would live only a mile down the road. Alice wanted them to live at their house so she could see her aunt every day. She knew not to beg or pout, but nonetheless, she did keep asking the question. Her mamm told her that they were building a love nest in the dawdyhaus for a little while. What bird nests had to do with anything, Alice would never know.

Gracie shed many tears saying good-bye to her dear sister-friends, Betty and Maryann. They promised to keep circle letters going. Since Betty had twins, she'd send recipes until she had free hands. Maryann said they'd call the yarn shop in Smicksburg from the phone shanty and leave Suzy messages.

Gracie received three rose bushes from Silas in early spring. A card was attached that said he'd always love her but in a brother sister way, maybe how it was intended to be. Silas knew her love for roses, and he wanted her to plant them around her new house when it was built. Silas said he was thriving in Holmes County, as were his parents and a few other families from Cherry Creek who joined them.

Their land behind Ruth and Boaz, where Gracie and Leander first kissed, was ripe with blossoms when building began. Leander jumped on his shovel to break ground for their new house, and then twirled

Gracie around, until she cautioned him that she was pregnant. But she took his sinewy hands and felt like dancing like a mockingbird.

# Book Club

## Discussion Guide

1. Who was your favorite character?

2. Which character showed the most spiritual and emotional growth?

3. Do you have a scripture to go to in times of distress?

4. Do you believe in love at first sight? When I met my husband, we felt like we'd known each other for years. But we waited three years to get married. Do you think it wise to write letters and visit like Leander and Gracie did?

5. Leander's character was inspired by my college roommate who had a port wine stain. She wore theater makeup, and no one could tell. However, when she showed her boyfriend her face without makeup, he broke up! How do you think you would react? How would you hope you'd react?

6. What do you think about Silas? Do you think he ever loved Gracie?

7. Gracie has a strained relationship with her sister, Rachel. Family dynamics can get testy.

Do you have a sibling or cousin you'd like to grow closer to? Is it worth the effort?

8. If you were in Gracie's shoes, would you share a million dollars among siblings? Give most to charity? I know an Amish man who was shunned after warnings that he made too much money. Some Amish rules are made to keep temptation at bay. What do you think about this?

9. Did you know about the differences between Amish groups? When I lived near Cherry Creek, New York, they only wore black and blue. An Amish man I bought apples from told me he'd be moving to Holmes County, Ohio, but not to tell anyone. He'd be labeled a 'liberal' Amish and wanted to skip town first. I respect the Amish in New York for not wavering on community rules. How about you?

10. Single Amish women don't live alone. This may seem strange, but it wasn't long ago that this was normal in America. Not only is it cost effective, but women were watched over for safety. Do you think we're too independent?

11. For an Amish family to have only one child is unusual. Do you think Abigail will eventually adopt or take in foster children as the Amish believe it's part of their Christian duty?

12. If you've followed me long enough, you know I love birds. Tim and I enjoy watching mockingbirds' display. It appears like their dancing, wings twirling about like

my granddaughter who's a majorette. A very cheerful bird to watch. The Amish are avid bird watchers. They have so many hobbies that cost little money. Can you think of a few things you can do that are fun and free?

# Recipes

## FUNNEL CAKES
- 3 eggs
- 2 cups milk
- ¼ cup sugar
- 3 to 4 cups flour
- ½ tsp. salt
- 2 tsps. baking powder

Beat eggs and add sugar and milk. Sift half the flour, salt and baking powder together and add to milk and egg mixture. Beat the batter smooth and add only as much more flour as needed. Batter should be thin enough to run thru a funnel. Drop from funnel into deep, hot oil (375-F). Spirals and endless intricate shapes can be made by swirling and crisscrossing while controlling the funnel spout with a finger. Serve hot with molasses, tart jelly, jam or sprinkle with powdered sugar.

## SPONGE CAKE
- 3 eggs
- 1 cup sugar
- 1 cup flour
- ½ tsp. salt
- 1 tsp. baking powder
- 3 Tbs warm water
- 1 tsp. lemon juice

Beat the eggs until thick and creamy. Add sifted sugar and beat well. Add water and lemon juice and beat again. Sift the flour, add salt and baking powder and sift again. Combine dry ingredients with the egg mixture, a little at a time folding in gently. When well blended pour into an ungreased pan with center tube. Bake in moderate oven (350-F) for 50 minutes.

# About The Author

Karen Anna Vogel has worn many hats: stay-at-home mom to four kids, homeschool vet, entrepreneur substitute teacher (aka survivor) wife to Tim for 43 years, musician. Writing has always been a constant passion, so Karen was thrilled to meet her literary agent, Joyce Hart, in a bookstore...gabbing about Amish fiction.

After her kids flew the coop, she delved into writing, and twenty-something books later, she's still passionate about portraying the Amish and small-town life in a realistic way, many of her novels based on true stories. Living in rural, PA, she writes about all the beauty around her: rolling hills, farmland, the sound of buggy wheels.

She's a graduate from Seton Hill University (Psychology & Education) and Andersonville Theological Seminary (Masters in Biblical Counseling). In her spare time, she enjoys knitting, photography, homesteading, and sitting around bonfires with family and friends.

Connect with her on Facebook. She loves to hear from her readers.

## Karen's Booklist:
*Check her author page on Amazon for updates*

AMISH KNITTING CIRCLE SERIES
*Amish Knitting Circle: Smicksburg Tales 1*
*Amish Knitting Circle: Smicksburg Tales 2*
*Amish Knit Lit Circle: Smicksburg Tales 3*
*Amish Knit & Stitch Circle: Smicksburg Tales 4*
*Amish Knit & Crochet Circle: Smicksburg 5*

STANDALONE NOVELS:
*Knit Together: Amish Knitting Novel*
*The Amish Doll: Amish Knitting Novel*
*Plain Jane: A Punxsutawney Amish Novel*
*Amish Knitting Circle in Holmes County*
*Treasures of the Snow*
*A New Song at the Amish Bed & Breakfast*

AMISH HERB SHOP SERIES
*Herbalist's Daughter Trilogy*
*Herbalist's Son Trilogy*

AT HOME IN PENNSYLVANIA AMISH COUNTRY
SERIES
*Winter Wheat*
*Spring Seeds*

*Summer Haze*
*Autumn Grace*


NOVELLAS
*Amish Knitting Circle Christmas: Granny & Jeb's Love Story*
*Amish Pen Pals: Rachael's Confession*
*Christmas Union: Quaker Abolitionist of Chester County, PA*

LOVE CAME DOWN AT CHRISTMAS SERIES
*Love Came Down at Christmas*
*Love Came Down at Christmas 2*
*Love Came Down at Christmas 3*

NON-FICTION
*31 Days to a Simple Life the Amish Way*
*A Simple Christmas the Amish Way*

CHILDREN'S BOOK
*ABCs with Peter Rabbit & Friends*

# Scripture Refelection

God so loved the world, that He gave His only Son, that whoever believes in Him should not perish but have eternal life. *John 3:16*

*God so loved the world*

*God loves you!*

"I have loved you with an everlasting love." — Jeremiah 31:3
"Indeed the very hairs of your head are numbered." — Luke 12:7

*That He gave His only Son*
*Who is God's son?*

"Jesus answered, 'I am the way and the truth and the life. No one comes to the Father except through me.'" — John 14:6

*That whoever believes in Him*

*Whosoever? Even me?*

No matter what you've done, God will receive you into His family. He will change you, so come as you are.
"I am the Lord, the God of all mankind. Is anything too

hard for me?"
— Jeremiah 32:27

"The Spirit of the Lord will come upon you in power, ... and you will be changed into a different person." — 1 Samuel 10:6

*Should not perish but have eternal life*

*Can I have that "blessed hope" of spending eternity with God?*

"I write these things to you who believe in the name of Son of God so that you may know that you have eternal life." - 1 John 5:13

To know Jesus, come as you are and humbly admit you're a sinner. A sinner is someone who has missed the target of God's perfect holiness. I think we all qualify to be sinners. Open the door of your heart and let Christ in. He'll cleanse you from all sins. He says he stands at the door of your heart and knocks. Let Him in. Talk to Jesus like a friend...because when you open the door of your heart, you have a friend eager to come inside.
Bless you!
If you have any questions, contact Karen at www.karenannavogel.com

Made in the USA
Middletown, DE
06 January 2025

68889619R00166